For Hughie
and Marlene
— and a long and
cherished friendship's

Love!
Jim

THE LITTLE PRINCE

A Reverie of Substance

TWAYNE'S MASTERWORK STUDIES

Robert Lecker, General Editor

THE LITTLE PRINCE

A Reverie of Substance

James E. Higgins

TWAYNE PUBLISHERS
An Imprint of Simon & Schuster Macmillan
New York

PRENTICE HALL INTERNATIONAL
London Mexico City New Delhi Singapore Sydney Toronto

Excerpts from THE LITTLE PRINCE by Antoine de Saint-Exupery, copyright 1943 and renewed 1971 by Harcourt Brace & Company and William Heinemann, reprinted by permission of Harcourt Brace and Reed Books.

Twayne's Masterwork Studies No. 150

The Little Prince: A Reverie of Substance
James E. Higgins

Twayne Publishers
An Imprint of Simon & Schuster Macmillan
866 Third Avenue
New York, NY 10022

Library of Congress Cataloging-in-Publication Data

Higgins, James E.
    The litte prince : a reverie of substance / James E. Higgins.
      p. cm—(Twayne's masterwork studies ; no 150)
    Includes bibliographical references and index.
    ISBN 0-8057-8372-5 (cloth)—ISBN 0-8057-8585-X (paper)
    1. Saint Exupéry, Antoine de, 1900–1944.   Petit prince.
  I. Title.   II. Series
  PQ2637.A274P465   1995   95-44329
  843'.912–dc20   CIP

The paper used in this publication meets the minimum requirements of American National Standard for Information Sciences—Permanence of Paper for Printed Library Materials. ANSI Z39.48-1984. ∞

10 9 8 7 6 5 4 3 2 1 (hc)
10 9 8 7 6 5 4 3 2 1 (pb)

Printed in the United States of America

For Jake

"... never could I judge what men might mean
Till I heard [him] speak out loud and bold ..."
(John Keats, "On First Looking into Chapman's Homer")

Contents

Acknowledgments

The frontispiece photograph appears with the kind permission of John Phillips/Musée de l'Elysée.

Special thanks to Nancy Vogel for her patient and professional assistance in putting the manuscript together.

Antoine de Saint-Exupéry

John Phillips/Musée de l'Elysée

Chronology

1940	Awarded the Croix de Guerre. Demobilized on 31 July. In December he arrives in New York.
1942	American publication of *Flight to Arras*. "An Open Letter to Frenchmen Everywhere" appears in the *New York Times Book Review*.
1943	Publication of *"Lettre à un otage"* (*"Letter to a Hostage"*) and *Le Petit Prince* (*The Little Prince*). Returns to Reconnaissance Group 2/23 at an American base in North Africa. After a crash landing, he is grounded.
1944	Obtains permission to fly five missions with his group now stationed in Corsica. Does not return from his tenth mission on 31 July. Recent evidence indicates that he was shot down by a German fighter and crashed into the Mediterranean.
1949	*Citadelle* (*Wisdom of the Sands*) is published posthumously.
1950	Posthumously awarded the Croix de Guerre.
1982	Publication of *Ecrit de guerre, 1939–1944* (*Wartime Writings, 1939–1944*, 1986).

LITERARY AND HISTORICAL CONTEXT

Chronology: Antoine de Saint-Exupéry's Life and Works

1900	Antoine Jean-Baptiste Marie Roger de Saint-Exupéry, born 29 June, at 8 rue Alphonse-Fochier, Lyons, France. Parents: Jean and Marie (de Fonscolombe). Two elder sisters: Marie-Madeleine (born 1897) and Simone (born 1898).
1902	Birth of brother, François.
1904	Death of father and birth of sister, Gabrielle.
1904–1908	Family divides time between their home in Saint-Maurice and that of their maternal grandmother near Saint-Tropez. Memories of this house are often included in Saint-Exupéry's writing.
1909–1914	Leaves day school in Lyons to enter a Jesuit boarding school, Notre-Dame de Saint-Croix, in Le Mans, where he is less than happy.
1912	Speed-racing pilot Jules Vèdrine gives the starry-eyed 12-year-old his first ride in an airplane.
1914	Archduke Franz Ferdinand of Austria is assassinated at Sarajevo, and the five major powers of Europe are plunged into war.
1915	Enters the Villa Saint Jean, a Marianist school in Fribourg, Switzerland, with his brother. Writes poetry.
1917	Death of his brother, François. Enters a boarding school in Paris to prepare himself for the entrance exam into the naval academy.
1918	Armistice, 18 November.
1919	Fails the second part of the entrance exam to the naval school.

1921	Inducted for a two-year term of compulsory military service. After flight training in Morocco, he obtains his military pilot's license.
1922	Continues flying, based at Le Bourget.
1923	Crash leaves him with a fractured skull and frequent spells of dizziness; it results in Louise de Vilmorin breaking their brief engagement.
1926	Death of his sister, Marie-Madeleine. His short story "The Aviator" is published.
1927–1928	Begins flying for the newly founded Latécoère Aviation Company under the supervision of Didier Daurat (the model for the character of Rivière in *Night Flight*). Becomes the director of the airport at Cape Juby, North Africa.
1929	Publication of *Courrier sud* (*Southern Mail*, 1933). Becomes the director of the new Aeroposta Argentina.
1930	Receives the Legion of Honor for his exploits while at Cape Juby, including carrying out several missions to rescue pilots forced down in the Spanish Sahara.
1931	Returns to Paris. Marriage to Consuelo Suncin. Publication of *Vol de nuit* (*Night Flight*, 1932). Wins the prestigious French literary award, the Prix Femina.
1933	Becomes a test pilot and nearly drowns in a crash into the sea.
1934	Goes to Saigon, doing public relations for Air France. Applies for a patent for a landing device.
1935	Reporter for *Paris-soir* in Moscow. Crashes in the desert of North Africa, attempting a speed-record flight from Paris to Saigon. He and his mechanic spend five days in the desert before their rescue.
1936	Reporter for *L'Intransigeant* on the Spanish civil war.
1937	Reporter in Spain for *Paris-soir*.
1938	Crashes again in a speed-record flight from New York to Punta Arenas at the top of South America. Suffers serious injuries from which he will never fully recover. During convalescence in New York he prepares the text for *Wind, Sand and Stars*. Made an officer in the French Legion of Honor.
1939	Publication of *Terres des Hommes* (*Wind, Sand and Stars*). In the United States wins the National Book Award and other honors. Returns to France and joins Reconnaissance Group 2/23 as a captain.

1

Historical Context

It is little wonder that Antoine de Saint-Exupéry spent his entire life with a deep desire for peace of body, mind, and spirit, for the time and circumstances of his life, along with his own deep sense of moral responsibility, afforded him few opportunities for rest. Born at the very outset of the twentieth century, he spent his childhood in a Europe still ravaged by bitter ethnic hatreds of ancient origin, continuing under the guise of national pride. Each nation had separated itself from its neighbors by setting up frontier barriers and arming for the inevitable conflict. And come it did. The boy Antoine not only was a witness to its horrors, but he also came to recognize, even at that early age, the futility of it all.

Following World War I, Antoine fell in love with flying, the profession that he would follow for the rest of his life. It would take him to far-off places like the Sahara and the Andes of South America. His early writing, which he looked upon as an avocation, focused on the ethereal joy he found in aviation—not only the joy of flight, but the pleasure of comradeship among pioneer pilots and the wonder of the air machine.

Meanwhile, however, the so-called civilized nations had again taken up arms and world catastrophe was on the horizon once more.

And when it came, Saint-Exupéry, despite all of his misgivings about governments, politicians, and generals, found that as a matter of conscience he must participate in the conflict that eventually would take his life. His final literary works, of which *The Little Prince* is perhaps the most enduring,[1] are his valedictory testament. These works are singularly remarkable because they were written not when he was detached and distanced from his wartime experiences, but while he was actively engaged in them. The enigma of Saint-Exupéry is that this most unusual man is at the same time everyman. He writes about adventures that few people will experience in their lifetimes, and yet ordinary people recognize in his writing a universal truth to which they can attest.

Saint-Exupéry was first recognized as a world-class writer with the publication of his books describing the pioneer days of aviation. *Wind, Sand and Stars*[2] is an autobiographical account of his travels and flying adventures, while *Night Flight*[3] is a novel depicting the dangers and difficulties faced by pilots like himself, who flew the first air-mail routes over the Andes. Both works are marked by a duality in narrative style that would become his distinguishing characteristic. In them the reader comes to know quite intimately a pioneer aviator who is fascinated as much by the wonder of a carburetor as he is by the forces of nature that he is struggling to overcome. At the same time this active participant in the machine age is contemplative, sharing with his readers his own deeply felt concerns about the soul of humanity, which seems to have been abandoned as a result of the fast pace and overriding materialism of a new age.

Saint-Exupéry employs this narrative structure in *Flight to Arras*,[4] in which he describes the hazardous air missions he carried out in the early months of World War II. At the same time, he makes an aesthetic attempt to answer the insults and vilifications of Gaullists because he would not join their ranks; but, even more important, it is in this book that he expresses his belief that the world will find no peace until a brotherhood is established recognize the responsibility of each for all, and all for each. He returns to this theme of spiritual bonding in *Letter to a Hostage*, an open letter expressing his anxiety for a Jewish friend and others, including his own mother, who were being held hostage in German-occupied France in 1943. In *Hostage* he once again looks beyond his own immediate concerns and experiences. He writes: "If I allow myself to be absorbed in party politics, I may forget that politics makes no sense unless it serves a spiritual certainty. . . . However urgent the need to act, we must never forget the mission that must guide our actions . . . We want to establish respect for humanity. . . . If such respect is rooted in the human heart, humanity will eventually establish a social, political or economic system that reflects it. A civilization is before all else rooted in its substance."[5]

It was at this time when things were going badly for France and the Allies, that *The Little Prince* came into existence. Through the writing process the immediate concerns and irritants that were consuming the author became the stuff from which his personal fairy tale emerged. Just as traditional fairy tales are representations of the collective psyche of a people who are continually adjusting to their social and physical environment, so does this more personal form serve the same purpose for the individual: the solace to be found in the fairy tale exists as much in the telling as in the listening. Here there is no need for a duality in structure, nor for rational argumentation. There is a religious quality about every good fairy tale that recognizes that people must sometimes reach beyond themselves, perhaps to the stars, in order to satisfy the holy hunger of the human heart. For the brief time that it took Saint-Exupéry to both write and illustrate this little book, he freed himself from being earthbound and wandered for a little while amongst the stars. The man of action rested briefly in the garden of his imagination.

The dialogue of *The Little Prince* goes directly to the heart of the matter. It is free of political correctness and the trappings of everyday history as recorded by journalists and commentators. Two individuals, each with strong opinions, meet, converse, and learn from one another. It is a cosmic encounter that in its own way reveals the nature of matters of consequence.

Critics over the years, but perhaps more often today, have displayed a tendency to associate authors with a particular group or school, emphasizing a trail of influences and similarities among its members. This, I think, is not the most productive way to consider the style and content of Saint-Exupéry. Neither as a child, nor in his mature years, could Saint-Exupéry be considered a student of litera-ture or authorship. A reader, yes, but one who approached books not with an eye for turning what he read into writing, but because he found in books stimulation for the mind and inspiration for the spirit. In his social life he often seemed uncomfortable in the salons of the lit-erary intelligentsia, and they, for the most part, looked upon him as an outsider—one who wrote about aviation. Curtis Cate notes: "When alone, he often read, but it was rarely a novel. It could be Plato or Aristotle, Bergson or Nietzsche, or some scientific treatise, for which he had an insatiable appetite."[6]

If one felt compelled to put Saint-Exupéry into a school, it would be existentialism. This is not to associate him with the writings of Sartre, Camus, Kafka, or Beckett, who would come after him and upon whom it is doubtful he had any real influence. For similarities in existential thought to be found in Saint-Exupéry, one should go back to its beginnings in the writings of Danish theologian Søren Kierkegaard. Although there is no evidence that he in any direct way influenced Saint-Exupéry, it was Kierkegaard who, a century earlier, told himself what he most needed was that which would make it clear what he must *do*, not what he must *know*; to find a purpose, God's will; to find a personal truth that will lead him to meet crucial situa-tions in an honest and responsive manner. This is as good a description as one can find of Saint-Exupéry's personal quest for a moral mapping that would help him deal responsibly with the exigencies of life.

Saint-Exupéry, like the existentialists—religious, agnostic, or atheistic—emphasizes man's responsibility for forming his own nature, stressing the importance of free will and personal freedom. In this scheme, it follows that the individual must rise above social, political and even moral conventions, to strike out on his or her own. Saint-Exupéry is concerned with man's essential being and nature, and con-vinced that thought and reason are of themselves insufficient to understand and cope with the mysteries of life. He emphasizes, too, the bitter realization that life, the act of becoming, is a painful journey and that anguish and feelings of despair are the lot of everyone. Nevertheless, it is the moral duty of the individual to actively and pos-itively participate in life.

Saint-Exupéry does not focus on the temporal time of the historian and the forecaster of human events; nor does he engage in looking for immediate solutions for current social problems. Indeed he displays a distrust, sometimes even a disdain, for those who express a conviction that events can be deduced each from the one preceding it. The past and the future hold little impact for him. His eye is on the continuous evolutionary unfolding of creation, which requires no time reference, for it is never completed, but always in the state of becoming. Even death, for him, does not halt the process. The ever-present of the existential *now* is for him the only perception of time that man can muster that in any way approximates the unfathomable notion of no time at all—God time—eternity. This is myth time, the time in which the hero dwells—the time in which exists the cedar tree, ever unfolding itself, from seed to tree and from tree to seed. His is the time of poetry, not history; the time of the philosopher, not the politician.

The influence of great thinkers can be legitimately linked to Saint-Exupéry's personal quest for his own moral imperative; but at the same time it would not be fair to say that he was a strict adherent to any one of their philosophies. In fact the ideas and schema put forth by the great philosophers are often in direct opposition to one another, as is the case with Pascal and Nietzsche. The common element that Saint-Exupéry found so satisfying in both was their vigorous exhortation that man should reach beyond himself for, if not greatness, at least goodness. Each presented his arguments passionately in the language of the poets. Their works were meant to touch the heart as well as convince the mind; and never did they shy away from the great mysteries that have forever puzzled humans.

The Sahara is more than the setting for *The Little Prince*. The years that Saint-Exupéry spent in that desert afforded him sufficient time and solitude for contemplation. From the vantage point of the Sahara he could look to the world he had left on the other side of the Mediterranean and see clearly that it was abandoning the truths so basic for the welfare of mankind. Not only the desert itself, but the people of the desert contributed to his finding a fresh perspective, a new way of looking at things and weighing their significance.

Once the little prince says, "I am responsible for my rose," the appearance of all things is changed for him, and because of this, all his actions take on new meanings. It is an assertion that illuminates the implications of another mystical statement that does not exhort, but commands people to love their neighbors. Saint-Exupéry recognized late in life that this commandment was at the very foundation of Western civilization, but that somehow it had been lost in the milieu of the twentieth century. There is quite a bit, too, in the substance and texture of Saint-Exupéry's thought, if one looks closely, that echoes a powerful voice that came forth from the Roman province of Numidia in North Africa during the fourth century—the voice of Augustine.

As mentioned earlier, *The Little Prince* was written while its author was personally dealing with the pain and anxiety caused by World War II. Saint-Exupéry was no stranger to warfare. His teenage years were spent amid the ravages of World War I in France, where so many of the battles took place. As a correspondent, he witnessed close at hand the horrors and atrocities of the disastrous Spanish civil war during the 1930s. He was an air combatant in France's futile attempt to stop the Nazi war machine. And yet, for Saint-Exupéry, the war itself, and the bestiality of the Nazis, was only a symptom, an erupting ulcer, that brought to the surface the insidious disease that had been slowly corrupting the spirit of Western civilization.

As to the matter of responsibility, he would not restrict it to one group, or to one set of circumstances. Looking beyond the ending of hostilities, he was pessimistic about the future. He is quoted as saying in 1943: "I hate this age. When this war is over, nothing but emptiness will be left. For centuries, humanity has been descending an immense staircase whose top is hidden in the clouds and whose lowest steps are lost in a dark abyss. We could have ascended the staircase; instead we chose to descend it. Spiritual decay is terrible" (WW, 139).

It is always concern for the human spirit to which Saint-Exupéry directs his attention. That is why this fairy tale, from among all of his writing, giving as it does flesh and animation to the spirit, best addresses that concern. *The Little Prince* asks its readers to turn inward, not outward, to find answers to questions concerning responsibility.

2

The Importance of the Work

There are several elements in *The Little Prince*, and facts concerning it, that are germane to considering its importance as a work of literature. Since these elements will be discussed at length in other chapters, however, I have chosen at this point only to list them, so that I may emphasize what is for me, as a teacher, the most important contribution that a book like this can make to the maturing process of its young readers.

First, then, to the list of the outstanding and enduring qualities of *The Little Prince*: simplicity of style and language; imaginative power; original motifs; grand themes. Its universal appeal is evidenced by the fact that it has been translated into 50 different languages and has found its way into films, television, stage productions, and other art forms. Furthermore, 50 years after its first publication, it continues to sell at a rate of hundreds of thousands of copies per year.

As a teacher I am very involved with helping youngsters discover for themselves that quality literature—both story and poetry—while it entertains, at the same time stimulates them to reflect upon basic questions relevant to themselves: Who am I? How did I get to where I am? What's it all about? I want my students to understand that literature, like all the arts, while it does not necessarily provide answers, does help its readers become aware of these fundamental questions, questions that are as relevant and significant for the young as for their elders. I want teachers, too, to see that one of the most important functions of the arts is to help all of us maintain our sanity in a world that often seems chaotic and without purpose.

It is crucial for developing readers of fiction to realize that while many of the stories they enjoy provide an escape from reality, there are others, equally enjoyable, that give them the opportunity to escape *into* reality. In their initial introduction to the library, for the sake of convenience and/or simplicity, children all too often are given a completely false definition of fiction. They come to identify stories as books of make-believe—which in itself is both accurate and valid, but does nothing to refute the essential *truth* underlying such works of the imagination. Honoring fact as the sole purveyor of all truth, many readers take this notion into adulthood, so that for them novels and such are considered books of little or no value. And when the work is one of a fanciful nature this false notion is compounded.

A work like *The Little Prince* is just the sort that may initially stir youngsters to begin to consider the connection between fanciful literature and reality; it may prod its readers to question the assumption that only the material and sensually experiential parts of life are "real." A reading of a book like this can be for some the first step toward understanding the power of symbolic language, awakening in them an appreciation of imaginative tales of fancy—ancient myths, legends, fairy tales, or their modern counterparts. Hopefully, as mature readers they will come to see that the truths of human existence can be expressed in different modes, both realistic and fanciful.

Let me here include a specific example to clarify the issue I've raised.

Any library catalog or subject index to children's literature will surely list under the heading of World War II *Diary of a Young Girl* by Anne Frank and *The Upstairs Room* by Joanna Reiss, but not *The Little Prince*. And this is appropriate, for subject indexes and bibliographies indicate only a book's plot, and where it is set in place and time. They convey information concerning the external elements of the story, not the internal workings of the author's mind during the creative process. And yet, if there is one important work in children's fiction to come out of World War II, it is this slender little volume by Saint-Exupéry. It was committed to paper while the author was suffering in mind and spirit, thinking of his loved ones who were trapped in occupied France, and while he was frantically trying to convince American authorities to give him the opportunity to return to combat flying duty.

Interestingly, *The Little Prince* is very similar in this regard to another classic fantasy for children that was first conceived when its author was mired in the trenches in World War I. At that time Hugh Lofting, a Canadian engineer who abhorred the cruel suffering inflicted on animals at the war front, created in letters to his two little girls at home, a character who so loved the animals that he was able to learn their languages. Thus came Dr. John Dolittle into the world of fiction. Both *The Little Prince* and *The Story of Doctor Dolittle* are founded in the actual experiences of their authors and reflect their deeply felt thoughts and emotions. On the surface they are entertainments, but underneath there is a resonance of quiet integrity that raises both far beyond the ordinary.

These two children's classics, though quite different in presentation, are similar in yet another way. Each aesthetically demonstrates the true powers of innocence, distinguishing it from naïveté and sentimentality. And, strangely enough, one will find humans in the history books of this century who have lived lives of extraordinary commitment identical in spirit to that exemplified by the protagonists in these tales of fancy.

Saint-Exupéry exhorts his readers to think with their hearts. Thinking with the heart does not produce sentimental slush; on the contrary, thinking with the heart demands commitments, avowals, actions. As we explore the text of *The Little Prince* in later chapters, keep this in mind. Keep in mind also how often Saint-Exupéry returns in memory to childhood in order to sort out for himself the complexities of life—to identify that which is of true consequence through the illumination provided by the eye of innocence.

Living proofs can be found who mirror the sacrificial extremes to which Saint-Exupéry's little prince will go in order to meet his responsibilities for those he loves. The author himself is a good example, but another immediately comes to my mind. Shortly after Saint-Exupéry had completed *The Little Prince*, and less than a year before he would make his last flight, there was in a London hospital a frail young French patriot named Simone Weil. She would die chiefly because she refused to eat while people in occupied France were dying of hunger. Weil, too, was very cognizant of the behavioral effect that great works of literature can have upon attentive readers. In one of her essays she makes the point more powerfully and succinctly than my attempt here. She writes: "they give us, in the guise of fiction, something equivalent to the actual density of the real, that density which life offers us every day but which we are unable to grasp because we are amusing ourselves with lies."[1]

It is paradoxical that one of the main reasons *The Little Prince* deserves its reputation as a children's classic is also the very reason that it gets very little space in texts about children's literature: its uniqueness. There are no other books quite like this. Scholars have found it difficult to drop this tale into a neat categorical niche, compare it to other works, or include it in their general commentary on works of fancy. It demands closer attention than their scope permits. And when they sometimes limit its audience to only discerning readers, they miss the point of what truly constitutes aesthetic education. How do youngsters grow into discerning readers, if not with the help of a teacher guide? How do they become engaged by a work that entertains at a higher level than amusement?

Saint-Exupéry does not write down to children. He is confident that they have the capacity to reach the literary plateau needed to enjoy and appreciate his story. He puts before them a book, written in simple and straightforward language, that dares them to reach down into their own experiential wellsprings to determine its relevance for themselves. He gives young readers the opportunity to ponder some of those mysteries of life and death, matters of consequence, in the face of which rote learning remains useless.

In *The Little Prince*, the author releases the secrets of his heart and mind through the simple power of metaphor. Explanation and argumentation give way to animation and drama. When youngsters see for themselves the simple procedure involved in the most basic tool of literature, they are well on their way to becoming discerning readers. The process is demystified.

Saint-Exupéry gives form to his anguish and feeling of separation from loved ones by creating the image of a little boy prince wandering through the cosmos in search of a friend. It is a story in which things are what they are, and yet at the same time the reader keeps wondering whether they are something else besides. Wondering is as essential to the reading of literature as is thinking, and it pushes thinking beyond the accumulation of facts and the limitations of logic. It awakens the imagination.

Some readers may not at first find *The Little Prince* to their liking, for it will require them to increase their tolerance for disturbance. It is a book that means to disturb, to bring into question certain values and notions. More important, it demonstrates quite clearly that one's beliefs require concomitant commitments and actions. Its importance as a piece of literature can be measured by the degree to which readers are drawn into their reverie of a pilot who has crashed in the Sahara, and who, after being rescued, finds his world forever changed by the experience. Similarly, to what measure will the readers' world look different to them once they have put the book aside? It is a contemplative work, linking as it does the child's perception of his own environs with those experienced vicariously through the act of reading.

The best art for children always possesses an element that arrests their imaginative attention. There is even an example of it to be found in the story itself. In the opening pages, after several attempts, the pilot finally draws a picture of a sheep that successfully meets the meditative needs of the small boy. The little prince at one point takes the picture out of his pocket to look at it, and then "he sank into a reverie, which lasted a long time. . . . [and] buried himself in the contemplation of his treasure" (14).

Parents and teachers who feel that children are not capable of such a literary encounter, or who are reluctant to exhort them to become personally responsible for themselves, their neighbors, and the natural world in which they find themselves, had best avoid acquainting them with a book like *The Little Prince*. I assure you, it is no sentimental journey.

3

Critical Reception

The genesis of any truly imaginative work is difficult to identify with any precision. Such works arise from a myriad of elements that somehow wind their way out of the author's subconscious during the creative process. Experiences of the distant past, some of which seemed to hold little significance at the time; people met; fleeting thoughts and images; dreams of both day and night—such a long list makes it virtually impossible for the author to pinpoint just where and when it all began. The best one can do is to recall when the specific writing project and the form it would take were initially considered by the writer, often in conjunction with a publisher or editor. In the case of *The Little Prince* these decisions arose during a luncheon meeting in a New York restaurant. Saint-Exupéry had made some doodles on a white tablecloth, featuring the small figure of a boy. When Curtis Hitchcock, his American publisher, asked what he was drawing, Saint-Exupéry replied: "Oh nothing much. Just a little fellow I carry around in my heart." Hitchcock then suggested that perhaps he might want to write a story, perhaps a children's story, featuring the "little fellow."[1]

This notion would probably never have entered Saint-Exupéry's mind, for even though he was already well known in the world of books, he still did not consider himself a writer by trade, much less one who would address an audience of children. Once the idea was presented to him, however, it didn't take him long to take hold of it. It is interesting to note that he began not with a writing instrument, but rather with a set of colored pencils. He consciously began to experiment with turning doodles into drawings—building upon spontaneous expression to create an aesthetic one. It would be the same with his writing: A close examination of the finished product indicates that the form of the fairy tale, and a story well suited for children, slowly emerges as the work progresses. The tale begins with a realistic (even autobiographical) tenor, then evolves into an ironic allegory that gently ridicules much of European and particularly American twentieth-century culture; finally, in the last half of the book, does the sad, and for some, tragic tale of fancy emerge.

Early reviewers had difficulty assigning a genre to this highly individualist work. Reviewers referred to it by several different classifications, each one having a validity of its own: fairy tale, fable, parable, allegory, satire, conte. In these reviews also, it was compared with the work of various "classic" authors. These comparisons, however, are always made in relation to only one part of the tale, never to the work in toto. The fairy-tale quality, for instance, has been compared mostly with the work of Andersen and Perrault—interestingly and aptly, never to the Brothers Grimm. One wonders why the fairy tales of Oscar Wilde were never mentioned—perhaps because Saint-Exupéry himself was not familiar with them. The allegorical and satiric quality remind some reviewers of Lewis Carroll, others of Swift, and still others of Rabelais. One must remember that in the year of *The Little Prince*'s publication children's literature had not yet become the vast enterprise it is today, and the works of such prominent writers as E. B. White, C. S. Lewis, and J. R. R. Tolkien were yet to come. Saint-Exupéry was aware of, and had a very high regard for, P. L. Travers's *Mary Poppins*. In any case, in its form *The Little Prince* is unique.

Though the form was new to Saint-Exupéry, the content was not. Once he began to write, the themes that surfaced were the same ones that had possessed him throughout his writing life. The mood and evocative quality of the work reflect not only his state of mind but his emotional condition as well. At the time he was deeply immersed in the writing and illustration, he was also fitfully trying to deal with the fall of France to the Nazis, his own self-exile, and the dark days that were surely ahead for everything and everyone he so dearly loved.

Probably the most difficult question faced by early reviewers, and one that is still repeatedly asked by adult readers, is whether this is really a book for children. This uncertainty seems to have been the main reason that some reviewers refrained from giving the work an enthusiastic reception: What makes any book considered good for children? Here before them was a book presenting little action, filled with satiric and philosophical passages, and ending with the death of the protagonist. Could a book like this hold the attention of children, and if so, could they fathom what it was all about?

John Chamberlain, in the *New York Times*, sums up his reaction to all of this in a final brief paragraph: "Anyway, *The Little Prince* will appeal to adults. And that is something."[2] Florence Bethune Sloan, though agreeing that adults more than children would find enjoyment within its pages, moves away from a consideration of the age of the reader and concludes: "If you like imaginative books, beautiful pictures in words, and in line and color, you will like the story . . . , whatever your age may be, and will fall under the spell of this enchanting book."[3]

For the most part, reviewers who ignored, skirted around, or minimized the question of the reader's age were much more enthusiastic in their reception. Like Sloan, they focused on the form of the fairy tale, suggesting that any reader who likes such fare would surely find delight in this one, despite its allegorical trappings. This is not to say there wasn't a minority dissent. Katherine S. White's review, since she found the story lacking in all aspects, is perhaps the strongest negative one: ". . . to my mind *The Little Prince* is not a book for children and is not even a good book . . . As a fairy tale . . . it seems to me to lack the simplicity and clarity all fairy tales must have in order to create their magic."[4]

On the other hand, in her review, Anne Carroll Moore, a preeminent children's literature critic of that time, rated Saint-Exupéry's contribution as "the most important book of many years."[5] Later on, in his biography of Saint-Exupéry, Curtis Cate raises the possibility that certain critics were "put off by the ironic digs at American civilization."[6] Yes, that is certainly a possibility.

P. L. Travers, whose *Mary Poppins* Saint-Exupéry thought the best children's book he had ever read, was the most enthusiastic of the early reviewers. She dismissed the matter of age altogether, and pointed out that *The Little Prince* possessed three essential requirements for a children's book: "It is true in the most inward sense, it offers no explanation and it has a moral." She concluded her comments with a most insightful sentence: "All fairy tales are portents and life continually reviews them in us."[7] For anyone interested, this notion about the portentous impact of story is examined at length by Graham Greene in his essay "The Lost Childhood,"[8] and in Travers's own address given to the Library of Congress, titled "Only Connect."[9]

Over the years, since the first appearance of this unique little book, critics have given it further consideration for a variety of reasons. A few have not thought it "too far fetched to suggest that parts of the story of the little prince are remarkably like a fairy tale transposition of certain episodes in the life of Christ."[10] Philip Mooney goes so far as to suggest that Saint-Exupéry "furnishes careful clues that identify the little prince as the boy Jesus."[11] There is little or no evidence to suggest that Saint-Exupéry had intended his protagonist to be seen as a Christ-figure, and yet there is validity in such a connection. Raised in the Catholic faith, Saint-Exupéry found as he matured that he could not accept on faith the divinity of Jesus; he nevertheless proclaimed unequivocally that Christ's message and his sacrificial offering of himself for his fellow humans were at the center of and in harmony with his own thoughts and feelings. Not too long before sitting down to write *The Little Prince*, he shared this personal revelation in *Flight to Arras*: "I understand now for the first time the mystery of the religion whence was born the civilization I claim as my own: 'To bear the sins of man.' Each man bears the sins of all men" (*FA*, 225). This theme, that each is responsible for all, blossoms in Saint-Exupéry's final works and ironically foretells of the commitment and sacrifice that the author would make for his fellows in the last months of his life.

André Maurois sees a similarity between Lewis Carroll's *Alice in Wonderland*, which "was at the same time a tale for little girls and a satire on the Victorian world and *The Little Prince* which . . . in its poetic melancholy contains a whole philosophy."[12] Robert Price likewise writes interestingly about the similarities between parts of *The Little Prince* and the fourth and fifth books of Rabelais's *Pantagruel*.[13] Laurence Gagnon, by associating pieces of Martin Heidegger's existential philosophy with certain aspects of *The Little Prince*, develops a model for interpreting its meaning and significance. The book's focus, he claims, is on the fundamental capabilities of the individual and the ultimate personal obligation of each human to endeavor to live a life of authenticity.[14]

Those readers who have read *Flight to Arras* and *Letter to a Hostage* will agree with Bonner Mitchell[15] who considers *The Little Prince* to be a conte expressing allegorically what Saint-Exupéry had already declared through exposition and direct argument. I will pick up on this idea in later chapters, as it reveals quite clearly what concerns were foremost in the author's mind and heart at the time of the writing.

In the 1960s I contributed two pieces to the growing body of criticism of children's literature. The first was a consideration of *The Little Prince* from the viewpoint of a teacher-librarian.[16] The second was a work that grouped Saint-Exupéry's little book with others that on the surface appeared to be quite different both in style and content—works such as W. H. Hudson's *A Little Boy Lost* and J. R. R. Tolkien's *The Hobbit*. The genre to which they collectively belonged I labeled "mystical fancy for children." Each work in this genre, I found, shares five qualities: they appeal to the heart; they are intuitively conceived; they reflect the reality of a spiritual world; they reach for a feeling of beyondness; they are marked by an atmosphere of joyful sadness.[17]

In biographies about the life of Saint-Exupéry, by such authors as Curtis Cate and Maxwell A. Smith,[18] readers will become more aware of the strong connection between the fanciful elements of *The Little Prince* and the author's own real adventures and experiences in childhood. Indeed, in all of his works, Saint-Exupéry exhibits the literary habit of resurrecting feelings evoked from his childhood years. In each book there is a hint or a foreshadowing of his "little fellow," or a reflection of the child he had once been.

Although she never specifically reviewed *The Little Prince*, no assessment of Saint-Exupéry's special qualities as a writer should fail to mention the contribution of Anne Morrow Lindbergh to a better understanding of his art. Anyone who has read the aviation works of each of these writers cannot help but recognize the remarkable similarity in their sensibilities. It goes deeper than composition; it resides in style, the manner in which each of them chooses to give form to the chaotic and enigmatic experiential world in which they find themselves. In writing about *Wind, Sand and Stars* in 1939, Lindbergh senses that another story concerning Saint-Exupéry's crash in the Sahara is still to be written. She writes: "One feels sometimes that the only great stories are those which are so simple that they are like empty cups for people to fill with their own experience and drink for their own need, over and over again, through the years. One thinks of the Bible stories, fables, the Greek myths, fairy stories, Homer."[19] Saint-Exupéry admired these same qualities in Lindbergh's writing, which he eloquently expresses in the preface to the French edition of *Listen, the Wind!*

In recent years, although its reputation as a "classic" continues to grow, there has been less consideration of *The Little Prince* as a children's book, than as a work best appreciated by adults and a limited number of discerning younger readers. Several of the newly published texts on children's literature used in American teacher preparation courses make no reference to it, while each of the two texts of long-standing use give it only a one-paragraph notation. *Children and Books* emphasizes that "the lack of action and the allusiveness of the dialogue" limit its appeal to young readers.[20] *Children's Literature in the Elementary School* recognizes it as a popular tale of our time for adults and children and in summing up it uses the word *gentle* as a description.[21] This interpretation, one with which I disagree, may be a reason that *The Little Prince* is sometimes found in gift shops, standing next to sentimental "inspirational" books, or pop-philosophies extracted from comic strips.

Saint-Exupéry continues to be of interest to academia, as exemplified by dissertations like Allen W. Davis's "Contradictions and Paradox as a Mode of Thought and a Stylistic Device in Saint-Exupéry."[22] An examination of recently published materials suggests that the enigma of Saint-Exupéry still attracts critics to a wide variety of his writing, and particularly to *The Little Prince*. Paul Webster in his biography, *Antoine de Saint-Exupéry: The Life and Death of the Little Prince*, identifies the prince as the child Antoine and puts forth the thesis that what distinguishes *The Little Prince* from the rest of his work is that he uses this "story to write of his inner distress over his marriage to Consuelo and the emptiness of liaisons with other women."[23] A quite different interpretation is put forth in *Discovering the Royal Child Within: A Spiritual Psychology of "The Little Prince,"* by Eugen Drewermann, a German psychologist and theologian. Drewermann writes "we will understand the central mystery of *The Little Prince*, the mystery of the rose, only when we focus our interpretation of it on Saint-Exupéry's mother."[24]

Barnet De Ramus, in *From Juby to Arras: Engagement in Saint-Exupéry*, considers the writing of Saint-Exupéry in comparison to that of Sartre, Camus, Malraux, and Hemingway. Although his position is that there is a strong connection between the author's personal experience and his writing, he does not include *The Little Prince* as one of Saint-Exupéry 's four major works, mentioning it only in passing.[25] Joy D. Marie Robinson's approach to *The Little Prince*, in her study of the life and work of its author, can be neatly summed up by her chapter heading: "Allegory and Apotheosis: *Le Petit Prince*."[26]

The issue of whether *The Little Prince* is suitable for children will undoubtedly continue to be considered by critics and readers alike. The sense of childlike wonder, innocence, and imagination, and the distinctive wisdom that emerges therefrom have certainly earned for it, after 50 years, recognition as a classic work of children's literature. It continues to sell at an annual rate well into the hundreds of thousands, and reaches people in 50 different languages. At this point in time, it is also possible to say of the final works of Saint-Exupéry, of which this is one, that they are books of prophecy, perhaps revelation. For indeed today we are witnessing what happens to societies when their people fail to recognize and seriously consider true "matters of consequence."

A READING

4

The Eye of Innocence

On first opening *The Little Prince* one should not ignore or pass over too quickly the dedication, for it also serves as a preface—briefly, but clearly, setting out Saint-Exupéry's approach to the narrative to follow. In the dedication he asks the indulgence of children, not adults, for dedicating the book to his friend Léon Werth, who at the time of the writing is somewhere in German-occupied France, hungry and cold. He refers to the work not as a children's book, but rather as a book "about" children. It is fitting, then, for him to emphasize that he is dedicating it "to the child from whom this grown-up grew . . . TO LÉON WERTH WHEN HE WAS A LITTLE BOY." And he, the author, in order to tell the story that only a few pages later he will describe as an overpowering mystery (10), will be required to go down into the essence of his own childhood. Memory, especially of friends and of loved ones, is an absolute necessity for him; loving remembrance preserves and nourishes the clear-sightedness he requires not only for his writing, but also for summoning up the courage for moral behavior.

To begin his tale he goes back in time to when he was six years old and came across an illustration of a boa constrictor swallowing an animal whole. The text accompanying the illustration is straightforward information. For the child, however, the picture is "magnificent" and so it overwhelms the text. It evokes within him a sense of wonder so powerful that he "pondered deeply . . . over the adventures of the jungle" (7). When reading, listening, or just looking, young children often transform ordinary informational material into dramatic representation. The wonder of their imaginations is stimulated by each confrontation with a new fact of life, moving them toward emotional involvement with each new phenomenon, until they become active participants in the facts of life.

From the outset Saint-Exupéry takes on a point of view that will demand of him the discipline to look out on the world of experience through the eye of innocence. In this tale the narrator does more than address himself to children; he speaks, as best he can, as one of them. In so doing he necessarily captures the attention of those adults who are willing to indulge themselves in the reading of a fairy tale.

Saint-Exupéry's return to childhood through remembrance is not self-indulgent, not an attempt to escape momentarily from the pain and confusion of adult experience. It is rather the best method at his disposal to capture the child's innocent state of mind—the manner in which children look out upon the world that surrounds them, and inwardly to the secret world of themselves, and sometimes even beyond themselves to the world of mystery and wonder. Plato said of this innocent state of mind that only a few are capable of retaining "a memory of the holy things they once saw"—and that even these few will have great difficulty in perceiving what it all means.[1] Writers like Saint-Exupéry, who write about or for children, do indeed retain an innocent eye, a childlike vision, and it is precisely because they do have difficulty in perceiving what it is all about that they create real stories, full of mystery and surprise, not moral or pedagogical tracts disguised as stories.

If innocence is thought of only as a childish state, a sort of preexistent virtue that slowly diminishes when one is faced with the harsh realities of the world, then there is little reason to pay much attention to it, outside of its psychological implications or as a matter of childhood ethics. However, if one considers innocence as a state of mind, a quality of the imagination that flourishes during the early years, one can well appreciate that through continued care and nourishment it can well serve the adolescent and adult in later years.

Rollo May defines authentic innocence as "a quality of the imagination, the innocence of the poet or artist. It is the preservation of childlike clarity. Everything has a freshness, a purity, newness and color. From this innocence spring awe and wonder. . . . It leads toward spirituality; it is the innocence of Saint Francis in his Sermon to the Birds. . . . It is the preservation of childlike attitudes into maturity without sacrificing the realism of one's perception of evil."[2]

One of the reasons, then, that Saint-Exupéry instinctively turned to the genre of the fairy tale was that in so doing he would necessarily address a child audience, no matter what its chronological age might be. The audience for the story writer is not merely the people who will buy a book after it is written, but the group, mute though it is, to whom the writer can speak during the lonely hours of writing. While in the United States doggedly trying to return to flying service in the war against Germany, Saint-Exupéry felt desperately alone, cut off from so many he loved who were living in occupied France. The adults he met were mostly concerned with matters of consequence for them: war bulletins, the stock market, golf, business, bridge, politics, fashions. His flying comrades were all dead: "I have not a single comrade left to whom I can say: 'Do you remember?'" (*WW*, 54). At another time he writes: "I need friends in whose friendship I can rest as in a garden" (*WW*, 131). And so it is to his hostage friend Léon Werth (when he was a little boy), and to those like him, that he turns to speak of those things consequential to him: the blueness of the sky, the love for an animal, the mystery of God.

For Saint-Exupéry, the difference between children and grown-ups is more a matter of outlook than one of age. The former able to grasp things by faith, while the latter rely upon reasonable evidence. Though he was speaking to a child audience, obviously he hoped that others would read his book as well. If it was meant for children alone, his task would have been easier. As he says, "I should have liked to begin this story in the fashion of the fairy tales. I should have liked to say: 'Once upon a time there was a little prince who lived on a planet that was scarcely any bigger than himself, and who had need of a sheep. . . .' To those who understand life, that would have given a much greater air of truth to my story" (18).

Lest the point be missed, Saint-Exupéry opens his first chapter by relating a childhood experience the aviator narrator had in his dealings with adults. When he was six, inspired by the illustration mentioned earlier, he drew a picture of a boa constrictor that had already swallowed and now was digesting an elephant. Grown-ups seemed always to see it as a drawing of a hat, so he next drew a picture that revealed the elephant inside the snake, "so that grown-ups could see it clearly. They always need to have things explained" (8).

If an adult couldn't pass the boa constrictor test, then he would "never talk to that person about boa constrictors, or primeval forests or stars. I would bring myself down to his level. I would talk to him about bridge, and golf, and politics, and neckties. And the grown-up would be greatly pleased to have met such a sensible man" (9).

Adults, for their part, advised him to give up drawings of boa constrictors and devote himself instead to the study of geography, history, arithmetic, and grammar. It is not coincidental that they fail to mention story, poetry, or any of the arts. The world of grown-ups is one filled with explanations, not explorations, ponderings, or spiritual adventures.

Saint-Exupéry wants his readers to find their way into the book. He asks of his readers patience and contemplation, cautioning them that this tale will not follow the ordinary rules of fiction. He realizes that writing that comes more from the heart than from the head will by necessity take on a different tone and structure. There will be ideas and notions for consideration, to be sure, but they will not carry an import equal to those mnemonic images that erupt spontaneously from the author's personal passions. He says: "I do not want any one to read my book carelessly. I have suffered too much grief in setting down these memories" (18). He already knows firsthand the loneliness of one separated from those friends and companions to whom he could speak from his heart. It is them, and others like them, children of the spirit like Léon Werth, whom he addresses when he writes: "for us who understand life" (18).

In order to avoid the pitfalls of polished prose and reasonable explanation, he picks up the box of paints and crayons from his childhood. He turns away from the art of words, which he has come to manage over the years with skill and sophistication, and sets to work drawing pictures, a process in which he still finds himself a groping novice. This shift affords him the opportunity to return to childhood, where he and the boy protagonist will be more closely attuned in thought, feeling, and behavior. With paint brushes in his hand he must, as he puts it: "fumble along as best I can" (19). It is not easy, for his new friend never bothers to explain anything, assuming that the aviator is like himself and therefore has no need for explanation. But the pilot knows better, for despite all of his efforts he realizes that at best he can only partially recapture a childlike point of view: "I have had to grow old" (19).

The little boy himself does not draw, but he is a good critic who helps the aviator, through trial and error, to meet what a child demands of a drawing. The pilot is first asked to draw a sheep, but each of his attempts is rejected, for one reason or another, with a gentle smile of indulgence. Finally, when his patience is exhausted, he draws a box with three air holes in it and declares that the sheep is inside. To his great surprise the boy exclaims: "that is exactly the way I wanted it!" (12). The boy has no problem with the drawing; as he bends over it, he looks inside and announces that the sheep has gone to sleep. Then it becomes possible for the two of them to take up a conversation about the sheep and why he is important.

When later in the story the little prince laughs at some of the rough drafts of the baobab trees, of which the pilot was so proud, and of the fox whose ears looked more like horns, the aviator replies: "You are not fair. . . . I don't know how to draw anything except boa constrictors." And the boy answers: "Oh, that will be all right . . . children understand" (80). It is then that the aviator draws a muzzle for the sheep, the significance of which will be taken up in a later chapter.

These illustrations are an integral part of the story. There are many instances throughout the narrative when the reader's attention is directed to a particular drawing, making it evident that the illustrations are not merely adornments. Like the aviator in the story, Saint-Exupéry did not pride himself as an artist, but he did find great pleasure in sketching, and this enjoyment is evident here as well. André Maurois, who was visiting Saint-Exupéry at the time he was working on *The*

Little Prince, observed how so like a child he was, eager to display his drawings to others the moment he completed one: "Saint-Ex . . . wrote all night long, calling us from time to time to show us his drawings: that planet so tiny that a single tree could disturb its equilibrium; and that mysterious boy-prince who was himself and yet was not himself."[3]

There is a tough delicacy in his drawings that makes them both childlike and most appropriate for this tale. Anne Carroll Moore described Saint-Exupéry's drawings as: "pictures so childlike and free, yet as suggestive of the ageless Primitives of the text, which, with all its fresh imagery and originality, is a reminder of Hans Christian Andersen and his supreme gift of giving life to the inanimate."[4]

Perhaps Saint-Exupéry comes closest to identifying the most significant characteristic of innocence when he explains why he is attempting to draw a picture of the little boy dressed like a prince, even though his efforts are crude at best. "If I try to describe him here, it is to make sure that I shall not forget him. To forget a friend is sad. Not everyone has had a friend. And if I forget him, I may become like the grown-ups who are no longer interested in anything but figures" (18–19).

It is enlightening to observe the intensity and seriousness of young children when they are busy at work with pencils and crayons. They instinctively try to capture the soul of the subject, and if the subject happens to be a friend, a pet, a loved one, so much more the effort. Their final representations may often have little resemblance to the material appearance of the subject, but their objective is always the same as it is here for Saint-Exupéry: to make the "portraits as true to life as possible" (19).

The illustrations continue throughout the narrative and beyond, the final one appearing with a note on an unnumbered page after the closing chapter. This illustrated epilogue consists of a childlike star appearing over two sweeping lines representing a horizon. The note reads: "This is, to me, the loveliest and saddest landscape in the world. It is the same as that on the preceding page, but I have drawn it again to impress it on your memory. It is here that the little prince appeared on Earth, and disappeared."

Unfamiliar as he is with the genre of the fairy tale story, Saint-Exupéry seems in the early chapters to fumble his way along, much as he has done with the drawings, trying to get the hang of it. The story (Chapter 2) begins just as any realistic tale might, and for those readers familiar with *Wind, Sand and Stars*, it could be accepted as autobiographical. Having lost faith in people who couldn't see his boa constrictor, the narrator says: "So I lived my life alone, without anyone I could really talk to, until I had an accident with my plane in the Desert of Sahara, six years ago. . . . The first night, then, I went to sleep on the sand" (9).

The reader is prepared for either a true-to-life adventure story, or perhaps a dream tale of fancy. However, at sunrise, which clearly indicates that this is no dream, the pilot is awakened by "an odd little voice. It said: 'If you please—draw me a sheep!'" (9).

He is astonished by the appearance of a little boy dressed in apparel fit for a prince. They are a thousand miles from any inhabited region, and yet the boy seems not to be "straying uncertainly among the sands" (10). And indeed, as the reader and the aviator will find out much later on in the story, the boy is actually on his way to keep a fateful appointment when the two come upon one another.

It will take the pilot, and therefore the reader, some time to learn more about whence came this alien child to our planet. The pilot will ask questions, but little boys, and especially little boy princes, are more accustomed to making requests than answering questions. In the case of a prince, naturally, the requests come more in the form of orders to be obeyed without question, and one should always assume that a prince's orders always concern matters of importance.

"If you please—draw me a sheep!"
"What!"
"Draw me a sheep!" . . .
"But—what are you doing here?"
And in answer he repeated, very slowly, as if he were speaking of a matter of great consequence:
"If you please—draw me a sheep . . ." (9–10)

And so the aviator and the reader must be content to find answers to the little boy's origin from information he casually provides during conversation:

> It took me a long time to learn where he came from. The little prince, who asked me so many questions, never seemed to hear the ones I asked him. It was from words dropped by chance that, little by little, everything was revealed to me. (13)
>
> As each day passed I would learn, in our talk, something about the little prince's planet, his departure from it, his journey. The information would come very slowly, as it might chance to fall from his thoughts. . . .
>
> This time once more, I had the sheep to thank for it. (19)
>
> Again, as always, it was thanks to the sheep—the secret of the little prince's life was revealed to me. (25)

The little prince has come from a planet no bigger than a house. On this tiny planet he spends some of his time cleaning out three volcanoes and finding quiet pleasure looking at sunsets; but the greatest portion of his time is spent caring for the one rose that grew on his asteroid. It is the love that the little boy has for this rose that will eventually become the moving force of the story, but there are other things that must be revealed first. The early chapters of the book satirically explore the world of grown-ups who have lost the eye of innocence.

The little prince has left his planet to relieve his loneliness and to search for friendship. His travels take him to six other planets before he arrives on Earth, in the middle of the Sahara, where he meets the flier. It is during these celestial visits that Saint-Exupéry uses irony to take humorous potshots at some of the absurdities to be found in the world of grown-ups.

On the first planet, he finds a king who immediately greets him as a subject. Of course the little prince wonders how he could be recognized, since he had never been on this planet. He has not yet discovered that the world is simplified for kings, for, to them, all persons are subjects. This is a kindly king to be sure, for he never orders subjects to do anything that they would not naturally do without his bidding. There is the same kind of gentle satire here that Seuss explores in *The*

500 Hats of Bartholomew Cubbins. For instance, when the little prince yawns, the king forbids him to do so, claiming that it is a breach of etiquette to yawn in his presence. When the boy explains that he cannot help it, since he has come on a long journey without sleep, the king bizarrely commands: "Ah then, . . . I order you to yawn. . . . Come, now! Yawn again! It is an order" (35).

During their conversation the little prince learns that this king believes his rule to be not only absolute, but universal. With but a single gesture he signifies the vastness of his domain: his planet, the other planets and all the stars. "And the stars obey you?" the prince asks. "Certainly . . . they obey instantly," the king replies. "I do not permit insubordination" (37).

It should be noted here that Saint-Exupéry himself was not in principle negatively disposed to kingship, nor to the concept of absolute rule, as evidenced by his posthumous work *Wisdom of the Sands,*[5] in which he examines the role of responsible authority. When the little prince asks the king to order the sun to set, the king demurs. "Accepted authority rests first of all on reason. . . . I have the right to require obedience because my orders are reasonable. . . . You shall have your sunset . . . this evening about twenty minutes to eight. And you will see how well I am obeyed!" (38).

Having no wish to offend the kindly old monarch, but seeing that there is no reason for him to remain, the boy asks the king to order him to be gone within one minute, since "conditions are favorable." When the king makes no answer, the prince takes his leave anyway. "'I make you my Ambassador,' the king called out, hastily. He had a magnificent air of authority" (40).

And so, as he leaves, the little prince comments to himself that grown-ups are indeed strange. It will not be the last time he reaches that conclusion.

On the next planet the prince meets a conceited man who, although not royalty, acts very much like a king. Here, the little prince is greeted not as a subject, but as an admirer, which in essence is very much the same thing. He learns quickly that conceited people are very poor conversationalists. They do not listen; they never hear anything but praise. Nevertheless, the prince does add a new word to his vocabulary. When the man asks if the prince truly admires him very much, the little prince asks him to explain the word admire, and is told, "To admire means that you regard me as the handsomest, the best dressed, the richest, and the most intelligent man on the planet" (42).

Having already observed that his companion is the only man on the planet, the boy immediately recognizes the absurdity of the answer. Baffled but undaunted, he quickly moves on, having gained a little more insight into the ways of grown-ups.

His visit to the next planet is an extremely short one. It is here that he meets a tippler sitting amid a collection of both empty bottles and full ones. Their brief conversation is essentially a parody of an old vaudeville routine. Asked what he is doing, the tippler replies that he is drinking. Why?—to forget. Forget what?—that he is ashamed. Ashamed of what?—Ashamed of drinking! And with that he ends the conversation by shutting "himself up in an impregnable silence" (43).

As he will demonstrate over and over again in the story, the little prince does not forget. He makes every effort to remember those barely perceptible things that are so often forgotten by others. It is in remembering that he is able to fit the jigsaw puzzle of life together. So many incidents that at the time of their occurrence seem trivial, unrelated, or insignificant, in retrospect are seen as essential parts of the story of life, giving it form and purpose.

It is only natural, then, that the little prince goes away puzzled, and with the judgment that the ways of grown-ups are "certainly very, very, odd" (43).

The visit to the fourth planet is longer, because there he meets a businessman who is very much occupied with counting—making it more difficult for the little prince to get answers to his questions. The businessman is up to the number 501 million when the prince arrives. When asked what he is counting, he replies: "Millions of those little objects . . . which one sometimes sees in the sky." No, not flies. No, not bees. Yes, stars. And when the new arrival asks what he does with all those stars, which he describes as little golden objects that set lazy men to dreaming, he is dumbfounded by the question. After it is repeated for him several times, he gives what to him seems a quite obvious answer: "Nothing, I own them" (45).

When the little prince mentions the similarity between him and the king he met previously, the businessman is quick to point out the essential difference between the two: Kings merely reign over things, while he owns them. A very different matter indeed. The little prince, of course, continues his relentless line of questioning. What good does it do to own the stars? To make one rich, of course. And what good does it do to be rich? It makes it possible to buy more stars.

Here young readers have the opportunity to contemplate the meaning of the word good, which they have so often heard in their lives, mostly in connection with their own behavior. To contemplate goodness is to contemplate purposefulness. The little prince's primary question is the same as the one instinctively and continually asked by very young children: Why? And of course, for those who encourage children to continue to raise such questions, no matter that the answers are not to be found in textbooks, the hope is that somewhere along the way amid their lengthy series of whys will come the most essential question of all: Why me?

The businessman gives the little prince a seminar on his concept of ownership. According to him, one takes possession of something by being the first to think about owning it. He owns the stars because nobody else before him ever thought about owning them. Once he takes ownership he administers them by counting and recounting their numbers. When the little prince argues that he cannot pluck the stars from the heavens, he replies: "No. But I can put them in the bank . . . write the number of my stars on a little paper. And then I put this paper in a drawer and lock it with a key" (46–47).

The little prince finds this very entertaining, but of little consequence. He informs the businessman that he himself is an owner. He owns, on his little planet, a flower, which he waters every day, and three volcanoes which he cleans out every week. He points out that it is of some use to the flower and the volcanoes that he owns them. The businessman, however, is of no use at all to the stars. Here the innocent boy lays bare the basic question concerning the ethics of ownership, and for that matter the ethics of sovereignty as well. He himself has not fully appreciated the import of what he has said; that will be brought home to him quite forcefully later on in the story when he meets the fox.

The businessman, mouth agape, can find nothing to say in response. So the little prince goes away with his view of grown-ups now becoming "altogether extraordinary" (47).

The next planet is the smallest of all. On it lives a lamplighter, and the planet has just about room on it for himself and one street lamp. The little prince feels sorry for the lamplighter because there was a time when he put the light out in the morning and turned it on again in the evening. He then had the rest of the day for relaxation, and the rest of the night for sleep. But now the little planet turns more rapidly and he has to repeat his work every minute. Though time has changed, his orders have not; so, being a man faithful to his work, he continues on, though there really is no need any longer for him to do so on a planet that has no people and not one house.

The little prince admires the lamplighter, especially for his faithfulness, but at the same time he pities him, for, by his own admission, the lamplighter follows "a terrible profession" (48). He truly regrets moving on once more, because the lamplighter is the first person he has met on his journey who thinks of something besides himself. The prince says of him: "That man is the only one of them all whom I could have made my friend. But his planet is indeed too small. There is no room on it for two people" (51).

An elderly and scholarly geographer lives on the next planet. After he has explained his work, the geographer asks the little prince to describe his planet so that he might take notes. When the boy mentions that he has a flower on his planet, he is told that flowers are not recorded because they are "ephemeral." In his inimitably dogged style of questioning, the prince asks repeatedly for the meaning of this unfamiliar word, until he is finally told that something ephemeral "is in danger of speedy disappearance." During the course of their interchange the geographer explains that he and his fellow professionals only record substantial things, "matters of consequence," like oceans and mountains: "We write of eternal things" (54). Eternity, thought of in terms of measurable, physical endurance is just one of the absurdities that fall suject to Saint-Exupéry's ironic touch.

More important, however, the geographer's definition of ephemeral has alerted the little prince to the vulnerability of the flower he has left behind: "My flower is ephemeral . . . and she has only four thorns to defend herself against the world. And I have left her on my planet, all alone!" (54). This is his first moment of regret for having left his home. Later, as he continues to learn more about matters of consequence for himself, this first flicker of regret will grow and intensify into a heartfelt urgent need to return. Indeed it will become the matter of greatest consequence for him, greatly overshadowing all others. Later, too, he will come to realize that his own body is itself ephemeral, since it, too, is in "danger of speedy disappearance" (54).

For now, however, he takes courage, and upon the advice of the geographer, decides to travel on and visit the planet Earth. Nevertheless, as he takes his leave he is "thinking of his flower" (55).

One can hardly explain away Saint-Exupéry's ridicule of the absurdities of adulthood by saying that he merely included it with tongue in cheek, or that he introduced it merely to tickle the funny bone of children. He has lingered too long for that; more than half of the book is spent helping the reader to see this world into which the little prince is descending. The simple revelation that he brings with him is made infinitely more potent by the paradoxical world of adulthood. It is actually the simplicity of the revelation when it comes that makes it mystical for the understanding of the adult.

Saint-Exupéry's life of solitude in the desert afforded him a great deal of time for contemplation, which finds its way into all of his writing, and no less here, in this fairy tale. From the vantage point of the Sahara, he could look back at the industrialized world from which he had come and see clearly that it was racing away from the simple truths so basic to the welfare of mankind—so basic, so universal, that they are experienced and accepted in childhood as well as remembered and understood by some few grown-ups. So if this is a tale on two levels, then for adults it is an enjoiner *to return to*, and for children *to hold on to*, those self-evident truths that somehow get shuffled away in the material complexities of a mad-paced civilization. Indeed, this deceptively fragile little story of fancy is in fact a bold portrait of the power of innocence that exists in the hearts of all people of goodwill.

Since here in the earlier chapters Saint-Exupéry is using the innocent eye of childhood to lay bare the foibles of adults, this tone contains a touch of both wry humor and mockery. He successfully juxtaposes the outlook of children with that of adults in order to ridicule the superficiality and wrongheadedness of the latter. His technique is similar to that of Mark Twain, who uses the innocent voice of Huck Finn to mock the social hypocrisy of his day.

At this point, however, young readers have not yet been emotionally engaged by Saint-Exupéry at the level they demand from their stories. The story is still more satire than fairy tale, and its ironic humor is best appreciated by more mature readers. In these early chapters one is reminded more of Voltaire's *Candide* than Wilde's *The Happy Prince*.

Before his own country was invaded and he and his loved ones were caught up in the anguish of World War II, Saint-Exupéry had already witnessed the horror and absurdity of the Spanish civil war. He came away from that experience both shaken and revolted by what he had seen, but despite the intensity of his feelings, he was nevertheless still a spectator, not a victim. And that is the level of engagement he has reached at this point in the story of the little prince and the aviator. Here he is engaged in commentary, with the world of adults as the object of his derision; soon his own personal anguish will draw him gradually into the story as a participant, and all humanity will be the object of his expansive sense of pity. It will be the rose in *The Little Prince* that will unexpectedly unleash the penetrating suffering of loss and separation that its author was experiencing at the very moment of the writing.

Learning to write *for* children doesn't come easily, chiefly because the adult writer seldom starts from *inside* childhood. As this story proceeds one can detect Saint-Exupéry gradually getting the hang of it, even though the style seems to be developing more from instinct than from a conscious method. Good writing is very much like life itself: one keeps working at something until, seemingly by accident, something triggers the component that had been missing all along. The rose is that component in *The Little Prince*, for with its introduction, the tone and substance of the tale change radically, love becomes the essential element, the satire fades, and a quiet tale of innocent tragedy begins to unfold.

One can cite several similar examples in the history of children's literature when an experienced writer, working on a children's story for the first time, suddenly discovers the powerful potential of the medium. In the case of E. B. White it was a little bird that somehow found her way into *Stuart Little*.[6] Stuart Little is a mouse born into a human family, and White makes the most of the humorous incidents that arise from such a nonsensical premise. His story moves along in a light and unassuming manner until the little bird Margolo comes upon the scene and immediately wins the heart of Stuart. When her life is threatened, she becomes terribly frightened and suddenly leaves without saying goodbye, flying north because that is where spring has come to the land. She leaves behind a devastated Stuart, who has not told her of his deep affection.

The remainder of the story, still filled with humor, relates Stuart's desperate journey north to find his love. When the story ends he has not yet found her—"But the sky was bright, and he somehow felt he was heading in the right direction." So, too, was the author. *Stuart Little* is indeed an enjoyable and satisfying book, but while writing it White was only beginning to appreciate fully the depth a writer like himself could reach in writing for children. He was now apprenticed in what was for him a new art form. It wasn't long after that he produced his magnum opus, a tale of love and friendship, *Charlotte's Web*.

In both life and story, when love arrives there comes with it, suddenly and unbidden, not only an increase in emotional involvement, but also a dramatic turn of events.

Another reason that Saint-Exupéry's story seems to begin with fits and starts, and with little evidence of what to expect in plot and theme, is that a true dialogue cannot immediately take place between an adult and a child, between a person who has already crossed over the invisible line of "experience" and one who has not. There must be a period of give and take while each tries to fathom what the other is trying to say. The aviator asks straightforward questions in his attempt to get information. The little boy, on the other hand, is relentlessly pursuing that which he perceives as essential to him, but he has not yet found the language to express it.

In the beginning, frustrated by the situation, the aviator is impatient. He wants to quickly establish a common ground so that a reasonable conversation can take place. He learns gradually, as do those parents and teachers who pay close attention, that impatience is fruitless. He realizes that he must allow the little boy to tell his own story in his own way. The boy is not responding to questions, because he is intent on finding words that will help him to explain the actions he has already taken, and to define the feelings he has experienced but as yet cannot understand.

William Saroyan, in his novel *The Human Comedy*, succinctly grasps the reality of childhood behavior. The small boy Ulysses, returning home from an adventure "out there" in the world away from home, sees his mother in the yard feeding the chickens. He goes immediately to the hen house, finds an egg and gently brings it to her, by which he means, Saroyan tells us "what no man can guess and no child can remember to tell."[7]

The symbolic importance of so many of these childhood actions is often missed by adults, who categorize or describe them as cute. Such actions are children's instinctive method of narration, the only nondiscursive means at their disposal to tell their story, to reveal what they are feeling at the moment. It is through the continued telling of one's own story that meaning in one's life begins to emerge. The myth-making child instinctively holds on dearly to self, and resists all external attempts to separate her or him from that self. It is almost as though children know better than adults the danger involved when one dons the cloak of adulthood, sometimes mistakenly called reasonable objectivity.

Wordsworth lamented for the children of his time, because the educators had taken their story power from them, and in its place had given them pseudo-stories designed to inculcate scientific knowledge, social dogma, and moral truth. In so doing they stripped children of the virtues of innocence, and the ability to focus always on matters of consequence.

Saint-Exupéry found the same fault with the educators of his day. He says to children at the outset of *The Little Prince*: "I have lived a great deal among grown-ups. I have seen them intimately, close at hand, and that hasn't improved my opinion of them" (8–9).

The pilot himself, having never forgotten his experience with the boa constrictor, comes to realize very quickly that he must not lead the little boy into a discussion of what he himself deems important, but instead must listen attentively and draw out when he can what the little boy is so intent on expressing. And so it is that he comes to learn one of the cardinal rules of good teaching.

At one point, when in response to something he has said the boy breaks into a lovely peal of laughter, the pilot grows annoyed, for he always likes his "misfortunes to be taken seriously" (14). However, as their discussions continue over the days he comes to love the sound of that laughter more and more. He comes to realize that the laughter of a child, like tears, is a language itself—a language that carries within it messages of far more import than could be expressed in words. It is also a language of lasting quality, because even six years later, the aviator still can find happiness at night because of the "sweetness in the laughter of all the stars" (89).

The final sketch of irony Saint-Exupéry shares with the reader concerns a Turkish astronomer, the first to see the asteroid known as B-612, which the pilot suspects is the very planet from which the little prince has come. When the astronomer first shares his findings with the international scientific community, he is dressed in traditional Turkish costume, so, of course, no one believes him. When he again addresses the same group after Ataturk has brought his people into the twentieth century, however, he is appropriately dressed in European-style clothes. Naturally everyone now accepts his report without question (16–17).

For Saint-Exupéry, adults are too often like Dickens's Thomas Gradgrind, who exclaims: "Facts alone are wanted in life. Plant nothing else, and root out every thing else. You can only form the minds of reasoning animals upon facts; nothing else will ever be of any service to them."[8] Saint-Exupéry puts it differently: If you want to speak to adults of a house you find beautiful, then you will first have to tell them how much it costs. Then, and only then, would they be able to estimate its beauty (18).

The house for the child, on the other hand, is more than its cost, more than its construction. The child has not yet removed the soul from the object. His sense of beauty is much more primitive; it goes much deeper than the facade of prettiness or material value. Children have an innate capacity to grasp the mystery of the house—to conjure up all the secrets a dwelling may hold, to reflect upon its history. They can attribute to the dwelling a life of its own. Its creaks speak; its shadows dance.

This innocent power of the imagination remains strong in a select group of adults, among them exceptional writers like Saint-Exupéry. In the words of Virginia Woolf, "There exists a group of writers who have a sense of the unseen. [It] may bring visions of fairies or phantoms, or it may lead to a quickened perception of the relations existing between men and plants, or houses and their inhabitants, or any of those innumerable alliances which somehow or other we spin between ourselves and other objects in our passage."[9]

It is common today to believe that the day of mythopoeia is with us no longer, but careful observation reveals that it is in the nature of humans to make myths. The dramatic fancy that creates myths is the raw material of both poetry and science. Children naturally create stories that they only half believe, stories that shape the world more to their liking. Storytelling is a conscious creative faculty within them. Its product cannot as yet be labeled art, but it is at least art's elder cousin, just as the child's lie is often the protective impulse from which the art of fiction emerges. Kipling speaks of this. So does Wordsworth when he proclaims that those adults who learn to take control of this faculty bring themselves closer to the world of angels. Thomas Hood laments the loss of this same faculty when he finds himself having crossed over the bridge that separates child from adult:

> It was a childish ignorance,
> But now 'tis little joy
> To know I'm farther off from heaven
> than when I was a boy.[10]

Talk of angels and heavens can find few listeners today, for it is now mostly confined to the theological disciplines; one finds little mention of such terms in discussions of the creative imagination. But whether one call it heaven, infinity, soul, or spirit, the power of the imagination is inseparable from the meaning of art. Saint-Exupéry sums it up well when he writes:

> I remember the games of my childhood—the dark and golden park we peopled with gods; the limitless kingdom we made of this square mile never thoroughly explored, never thoroughly charted. We created a secret civilization where footfalls had meaning and things a savor known in no other world.
>
> And when we grow to be men and live under other laws, what remains of that park filled with the shadows of childhood, magical, freezing, burning? What do we learn when we return to it and stroll with a sort of despair . . . marvelling that within a space so small we should have founded a kingdom that had seemed to us infinite—what do we learn except that in this infinity we shall never again set foot, and that it is into the game and not the park that we have lost the power to enter? (*WSS*, 168–69)

The chief quality that is necessary for a good reading of *The Little Prince* is an instantaneous and calm acceptance of mystery. This is one of those rare books that leave the reader always wondering what it is all about. Some readers, young and old, may not be pleased by such ambiguity, for a book that evokes wonder is also sure to stir up a bit of confusion—and confusion, for these particular readers, is an intolerable disturbance to both mind and spirit. All of Saint-Exupéry's writing seems to be prefaced by "I wonder," and *The Little Prince* is no exception. It is a quiet adventure into the realm of the spirit, and therefore it demands readers who are not only willing to be disturbed, but eager to set forth on a journey into unchartered ways.

How often after reading a book like this will an adult say: "But will children understand it?" And by so doing they immediately place a criterion upon the work that is not appropriate to its nature. Many readers give up reading fairy tales at a very early age under the pressure of an adult environment that constantly stresses the "here and now." They come to believe that such tales are beneath their intelligence, that it is a waste of time to read a story that fails to reproduce the scientific facts of the "real world."

The genre of the fairy tale first attracted Saint-Exupéry's attention because it provided the form in which he could best encompass the thoughts, feelings and images that he wished to express. It gave him a playing field to manifest the wonder that possessed him. The fairy tale as such, however, is no more appropriate for children than for adults. In this little book Saint-Exupéry succeeds in doing what few writers have been able to do: he captures the innocence of childhood. When adults come away from *The Little Prince* wondering whether children are capable of grasping its meaning, they are in truth missing the essence of the story. They are assuming that Saint-Exupéry has written an allegory or a myth that permits the child reader to become engrossed in the story, while adult readers are free to busy themselves with meanings that lie beneath the narrative surface. While it is true that *The Little Prince* is satirically allegorical when it examines the ways of adults in the early chapters, that is not the heart of the book. If it must be categorized, then it is best classified as a story *filled with mystery*, rather than as myth or allegory, and the mystery should fruitfully perplex the adult as well as the child.

This is not a mystery in the sense that modern readers have come to know the term—the type of mystery that excites the rational curiosity of the detective or the scientist. It is, rather, a mystery wrapped in the cloak of innocence—a mystery that excites both awe and wonder when a secret of the heart is revealed. It is a mystery whose meaning lies not in the answers it provides, but in the wonder it evokes.

In this chapter I have attempted to demonstrate that Saint-Exupéry did not lose the power to play the game that takes one outside the limits of man's conception of space and time. My intent has been to introduce the reader to Antoine de Saint-Exupéry, the man as well as the writer. In his case, more than for any other author I know, the man of action and the contemplative writer are identical. His books are simultaneously tales of adventurous odysseys and spiritual pilgrimages. In his public life he often chose the more difficult path by rejecting that which others thought he should follow and, by heeding his conscience, did what he had to do. There were indeed particular incidents in his life that were of such a dramatic nature that they became indelibly imprinted upon his memory. When his creative imagination was at work these memories came forth in a variety of metaphors. In many cases his memories were acutely painful: the death of his younger brother when they were yet children, his plane crash in the Sahara, his flight over war-torn Arras. There were also memories, however, of fleeting moments of the peace he so desired, such as the day he spent with his friend Léon Werth on the banks of the Saône.

In the next chapters I will endeavor to illustrate how Saint-Exupéry's use of symbol in *The Little Prince* springs not from an imagination that roams in the abstract, but one that penetrates the material world in order to reveal the spirit of things. It is work best done by one who possesses the eye of innocence, for he will hold nothing back. Anyone who reads *The Little Prince* carefully comes to know instinctively its author. He truly lays bare his heart and soul for all to see.

5

The Landscape of Metaphor

Antoine de Saint-Exupéry was happiest when he was seated behind the controls of an airplane during the pioneer years of aviation. He flew over much of the world and helped to inaugurate airmail routes in places such as North Africa and South America. Perhaps better than anyone else, he captured in words the exhilarating experience of man's adventures in the air. It is not his flying experiences that I want to treat in this chapter, however, but his love affair with Earth.

The thousands of solo hours that early fliers spent in small aircrafts, flying at low altitudes, afforded them a look at Earth's landscape that had never before been experienced. This bird's-eye view of the forests, the mountains, the deserts, the waters, combined with the swift movement of the ever-changing panorama stimulated Saint-Exupéry's imagination, awakening his metaphoric urge to fuse matter with spirit. His cockpit was for him a mystical chamber from which he could see nature as Blake saw it, "not with but through the eye."[1] It is a view that seems to bring with it a glimpse of spiritual truths. With this vision as a base, he added the other basic tools of the poet—smell, touch, and taste—to create a rich symbolic world.

The symbolism in Saint-Exupéry's work is not a series of abstract ciphers to be analyzed and decoded by the intellect, nor a means of strengthening the singular vision of the logician. Like life itself his symbols are often ambiguous, sometimes enigmatic, their meaning never totally revealed or explained.

The symbols in *The Little Prince* are not the allegorical constructs one finds in most other modern fairy tales; they are instead connecting links between this tale of fancy and the author's own life experiences, including those he had already described realistically in earlier works. All of the natural objects that find their way into *The Little Prince* have already been sensually experienced by the author: they have touched his life, they have substance and poignancy. Their meaning is not something beyond themselves. True, as presented, they take the reader strangely beyond material reality, but not beyond the contact of spirit that sometimes, and in the case of Saint-Exupéry often, takes place between the human subject and the natural objects of his or her environment. They are more than figments of the imagination; they are objects of reality whose meaning is grasped by one who possesses an exceptional imagination and a gifted way with words, one who has pondered for a lifetime the question of essence, existence, and purpose.

As Saint-Exupéry says in *Flight to Arras*, "Man's spirit is not concerned with objects; that is the business of our analytical faculties. Man's spirit is concerned with the significance that relates objects to one another. With their totality, which only the piercing eye of the spirit can perceive" (29–30).

THE DESERT

During his life as an aviator Saint-Exupéry had many accidents, but none so life-threatening as his 1935 crash in a remote region of the North African desert, during an attempt to set a speed record from Paris to Saigon. This experience, when he wandered in the desert for five days with practically no water before being rescued by a Bedouin on a slow-moving camel, is vividly described in his autobiographical *Wind, Sand and Stars*.

And now, in *The Little Prince*, the same experience is lived once more, but this time the elements of nature form a metaphoric doorway into the world of the spirit—the world that lies hidden beneath the surface of things, but that nevertheless holds the secret key for understanding their meaning. If he had not actually wandered thirst-quenched for days in the Sahara, it is doubtful that Saint-Exupéry could have brought so much reality of the spirit to this fantastic tale.

Until the pilot of the story crashed, the desert had been for him, as it is for many others, a source of meditative wonder and beauty. He was merely a detached observer of the panoramic beauty of dunes and hillocks—serene and expansive. He also had leisure time at his disposal for his churchlike meditation. Now, however, he is suddenly thrust into a menacing environment. The desert is no longer serene and detached. He is now a part of the landscape and an active participant in a drama of life and death.

In this setting the beauty does not fade away, but in a strange way it is heightened. The beauty of things now exists in their actual being, rather than in what they seem to be. Here is action, drama, tragedy, fate, and destiny. Here is the stuff of which the fairy tale is made: odor, sound and sight, taste and touch.

The aloneness of the desert is not frightening for the pilot, only different. In the opening pages he admits that he had always felt alone in spirit while in the world of people. "I lived my life alone, without anyone that I could really talk to" (9). So from the very outset it is evident that the pilot finds himself by fateful accident in the same place to which the little prince has come with clear purpose and resolve. When the little prince first touches Earth and finds no people, he becomes afraid that he has come to the wrong planet—for after all, it is friendship that he seeks. He is told by a snake, the first creature he encounters, that he is in the desert where there are no people. The boy comments that it is "a little lonely in the desert"—to which the snake replies, "It is also lonely among men" (58).

There is a discipline of the spirit that comes with an aloneness free from the need to respond to the constant chattering of others. The mind is left free to respond to those elements of existence that go beyond the realm of abstract ideas. In order to commune with the world of nature, to hold discourse with its forces, one must direct not only the mind, but the heart and soul to the conversation. The poet is not content to stand by in the role of the dispassionate observer, but takes a step to become simultaneously both part of the experience and its recorder.

The picture of this vast desert, a thousand miles from any inhabited region, also emphasizes the fact that humans only "occupy a very small place upon the Earth" (57). Here the false notion that humans are the center of importance is reduced to its proper perspective. Oddly, this realization doesn't negatively effect either of the two central characters. The dialogue between the two, as well as their individual musings, indicates that they are induced by the environment and circumstances to a higher plane of visionary thought. In other works, Saint-Exupéry often referred to this state as dreaming. It is not the dreams of sleep he refers to, but what is most often called daydreaming—individual moments of heightened awareness.

It is in these heightened moments that memory of the holy things already experienced in the innocence of childhood return, unbidden, and cast a fresh flash of significance over the immediate experience of the adult. The insignificant elements of the immediate are cast away, leaving only the essential, that which is invisible to the anatomical eye, but radiant to the eye of the soul.

When the little prince says that the desert is beautiful, the pilot inwardly affirms his observation. Then the little prince adds that what makes the desert beautiful is that somewhere it hides a well. And suddenly the pilot is astonished by a sudden understanding of the mysterious radiation of the sands. He makes an instantaneous metaphoric connection to the house of his childhood: "When I was a little boy I lived in an old house, and legend told us that a treasure was buried there. To be sure, no one had ever known how to find it; perhaps no one had ever even looked for it. But it cast an enchantment over that house. My home was hiding a secret in the depths of its heart" (76).

And so he discovers that which he had already known, but at the same time had not known: that what gives things their beauty is something invisible. Ironically, it is the nothingness of the desert that leads him inevitably to the secret of everything.

For the genesis of this scene one can go to Saint-Exupéry's *Wind, Sand and Stars*, where in the midst of realistic prose he instinctively reaches for the language of the fairy tale in order to express this secret of the heart. Lost in the desert with little hope that he will be found, he experiences a peaceful bliss in dreaming about this same old house of his childhood that he so loved. He comes then "to discover of what absences the savor of this desert was composed . . . the origin of the feeling of eternity that came over me in this wilderness" (*WSS*, 108–9).

WATER

A thing is best appreciated in a setting where it is both scarce and essential. When the pilot crashes in the desert, it is his small supply of water that first gets his attention: "It was a matter of life for me: I had scarcely enough drinking water to last a week" (9). The symbolic power of water in *The Little Prince* arises from the tension between the aviator's realistic understanding of the desert environment and the boy prince's metaphoric connection between the thirst for water and the thirst for friendship.

During his time among the people of the Sahara, Saint-Exupéry came to understand their reverence for nature, and particularly for water, which they regarded as a blessed gift from God. In *Wind, Sand and Stars* he remembers that some Bedouins, given the rare opportunity to visit France, were not much impressed by Paris and the Eiffel Tower, but the French Alps were another matter. Their guide brought them to the site of a tremendous waterfall, and when, after a while, he suggested that they leave, they would not stir.

> "Leave us here a little longer."
> They stood in silence. Mute, solemn, they had stood gazing at the unfolding of a ceremonial mystery. . . .
> "That is all there is to see," their guide had said, "Come."
> "We must wait."

"Wait for what?"
"The end." (*WSS*, 142–43)

In all their previous imaginings they could not possibly conceive of any people on earth being so fortunate as to have such an abundance of this blessed element.

To truly teach someone to appreciate the beauty and goodness of water, one must first teach him to thirst. Similarly, it is said, if you would have someone repent his ways, it is best not to lay guilt upon his conscience, nor warn him of the punishments that follow such behavior, but rather to help him crave goodness, to feel loss rather than guilt. And so too, if you would teach children to care for the natural world in which they find themselves, do not fill their heads with statistics and warnings about the dire results of misuse of the environment, but rather help them to know better the things of nature so that their intuitive love for all creation will be nourished and continue to grow. One cannot learn to care for (or as the fox would say, "tame") anything without first learning to love it. Teaching others to love is not, as some educators would say, a false, sentimental, and unpragmatic approach to life, but rather one that fiercely, bravely, and naturally faces the realities of human existence—accepting pain with pleasure, and ultimately discovering the joy or bliss that comes only to those who have suffered.

The little prince has set forth on his long and dangerous journey because his thirst for friendship is also a matter of life and death. But this is not evident to the pilot, who says to himself, "He has no way of guessing the danger, . . . He has never been hungry or thirsty." So when the boy suggests that they look for a well, the pilot, who is too tired to argue with this naive proposal, sets out with him, even though he thinks it absurd to look for a well in the immensity of the desert (75).

In his other writings Saint-Exupéry often used analogies and similes to emphasize a point, or to get beneath the material surface of things. Here in this story of fancy, however, the "is like" of simile gives way to the much more powerful imagery of metaphor. The spiritual power of the symbol of the well is emphasized because when they find it, it is not merely a hole dug in the sand, like the typical wells of the

Sahara; it is a fairy tale well. The pilot thinks he must be dreaming. It is like a village well with everything "ready to use: the pulley, the bucket, the rope" (78).

After the pilot hoists the bucket slowly to the edge of the well and sets it there, he is tired but happy about his achievement. The song of the pulley still rings in his ear. It is then that the little prince says: "I am thirsty for this water." And the pilot finally understands what the little boy has been looking for all along: "This water was indeed a different thing from ordinary nourishment. Its sweetness was born of the walk under the stars, the song of the pulley, the effort of my arms. It was good for the heart, like a present" (78–79).

And again he makes an immediate dream-connection to an earlier experience of childhood: "When I was a little boy, the lights of the Christmas tree, the music of the Midnight Mass, the tenderness of smiling faces, used to make up, so, the radiance of the gifts I received" (79).

Some readers, more adults than youngsters I would suspect, might mistakenly term such recall of childhood experiences as pure sentimentality. If so, they are far off the mark. The spirit of Christmas experienced by so many children all over the world—and adults who can remember from *inside* their childhood—is very real. Its realness, however, is somehow best captured by dreamlike stories—fairy tales, if you will, like Dickens's *A Christmas Carol*, and *The Little Prince*.

This experience at the well is remembered during the last moments of the story, and again when the two who have become friends are parting forever. The little prince leaves the aviator a gift that will permit him always to hear laughter whenever he looks at the stars, but he also takes as a gift for himself a remembrance of the well: "Because of the pulley, and the rope, what you gave me to drink was like music. You remember—how good it was" (84).

And at the very end he mentions how the stars will be their contact in the future: "You know, it will be very nice. I too shall look at the stars. All the stars will be wells with a rusty pulley. All the stars will pour out fresh water for me to drink" (87). And later, "I shall have five hundred million springs of water" (88).

Earlier, in *Letter to a Hostage*, Saint-Exupéry also speaks of water as a means to quench the thirst of the heart. Remembering his rescue in the desert after his near-fatal crash, he says: "Water has no power of enchantment unless it is a gift of human goodwill. The care of a patient, the welcome given to a fugitive, forgiveness itself, are only worthwhile because of the smile that goes with them. We meet in a smile above language, party politics, castes" (*WW*, 116).

Like all good fairy tales, the story of *The Little Prince* goes on even after words are ended. The pilot and the boy each live happily ever after. Their thirst is to be forever quenched, because each has given himself to the other in friendship.

THE SNAKE

It is not a human that the prince first encounters when he arrives on Earth, but rather "a coil of gold, the color of moonlight . . . a snake" (57)—one of the deadly vipers that inhabit the Sahara. Their encounter is brief, but when they part the reader knows that they will meet again, and the inevitability of this future meeting changes the mood of the story. Indeed, a new story begins. The child reader is introduced to a tale of tragedy—not the wild emotional tragedy of adulthood, with the hero struggling valiantly but hopelessly against inexorable forces, but rather a calm, innocent, even melancholic, acceptance of fate. Its essence is the realization that everything that lives in nature will die. And so the tale takes on a circular shape as the reader realizes that this point must be returned to. The reader may wish to deny this inevitability, but in the end it must be accepted. The little prince, like the child reader, knows that he will meet the snake again, and he both wishes and fears it.

Of course, the trappings of a story in which a little prince descends to Earth and converses with a serpent, inevitably suggests allegory. In this case, however, such a suspicion is groundless. This snake is but a creature of nature playing out its intended role in the scheme of things. At the same time, it is the creature whose presence always lends itself appropriately to the arena of mystery, to the tale filled with secrets. Out of the secret confines of the earth comes this strangely beautiful creature with cold metallic skin and a forked and flickering tongue, gliding silently over the earth—an image that has always fascinated humans, especially the young. The snake is one of the few things in the world that, when beheld, invite the touch because of their mysteriousness, yet make one fear the touch because of its differentness. It is "Snake," by D. H. Lawrence:

> And truly I was afraid, I was most afraid,
> But even so, honoured still more,
> That he should seek my hospitality,
> From out the dark door of the secret earth.[2]

The snake is an allusive symbol rather than an allegorical one, inducing within the reader a particular *feeling*, which in turn makes it possible for him or her to share intuitively the spiritual experience of the protagonist.

The conversation between the prince and the snake takes up little more than one page, and yet it has an immediate impact on the reader. A tension arises because the reader becomes suddenly aware that the possibility of death is close at hand, while the little prince seems not to understand the danger at all. When the prince says that he is disappointed not to find men in the desert, and that it makes him lonely, the snake gives him the first hint that he may have no more success in his quest for friendship on Earth than he has had on any other planet. He says, "It is also lonely among men" (58).

Having never seen a snake before, the little prince playfully remarks that he finds him to be "a funny little animal." In response the snake makes metaphorical references to his power, ending with the calm statement: "Whomever I touch, I send back to the earth from whence he came." There is no resonance of evil or retribution in his voice: his is simply the power of inevitability. The little prince moves the snake to pity because of his innocence. He makes a strange offer of assistance: "I can help you, some day, if you grow too homesick for your own planet." When he attempts to explain further, the boy interrupts him: "Oh! I understand you very well. . . . But why do you always speak in riddles?" (59).

The power of innocence is the power to grasp the simple truth, be it pleasant or not. The innocence of the little prince must not be mistaken for naïveté. Though the snake uses metaphor to describe its power to end life, the boy understands him perfectly. Here, in this fairy tale, Saint-Exupéry accomplishes what parents and teachers, often without success, have been attempting for generations: to explain the meaning of death to children. He sheds light on the wonder and mystery of the experience, recognizing that all true mysteries are accompanied by a natural fear of the unknown.

The second and final meeting with the snake will be taken up in a later chapter.

THE BAOBABS

One of the narrator's few direct remarks to the reader concerns the baobab trees. "Perhaps you will ask me, 'Why are there no other drawings in this book as magnificent and impressive as this drawing of the baobabs?'" His reply is simple. In the case of the baobabs, he was carried beyond himself "by the inspiring force of urgent necessity" (24).

Here on Earth, the baobab is a tree native to tropical Africa, and it has properties that are very useful to man, especially for medicinal purposes. It is also one of the largest trees in the world, growing from 40 to 60 feet high, with a trunk that often measures 30 feet in diameter and a branch spread of another 30 feet. Therefore, if even one baobab were permitted to grow beyond a seedling on the little prince's tiny asteroid B-612, it would cause a total disaster. So within the confines of this story Saint-Exupéry consciously includes them as symbols of evil when considering the welfare of the little prince's home planet. In doing so he again demonstrates that the innocent eye is not naively blind to present dangers, nor to the need to take action. At the same time he includes an element of relativity in considering the danger concerning the baobabs.

A reader should not be put off by Saint-Exupéry's use of the childlike word *bad* in place of the more sinister word *evil*. The seriousness of the matter is not diminished because it is presented in a child's vocabulary. In fact the scope of the problem is made more universal because the author dares to include children in the discussion: There are "on the planet where the little prince lived—as on all planets—good plants and bad plants" (20). These plants, or course, come from seeds that lie invisible in the earth's darkness, and when they first meet the light of day it is difficult to distinguish the good from the bad. Yet, the little prince recognizes the need to regularly pull up the baobabs as soon as he can distinguish them from the rose bushes they resemble so closely in their early stages. Admittedly it is tedious work, but work that cannot be put off until tomorrow: "A baobab is something you will never, never be able to get rid of if you attend to it too late. It spreads over the entire planet. . . . And if the planet is too small, and the baobabs are too many, they split it in pieces" (21).

The pilot admits that on Earth he and his friends have been skirting this issue for a long time. One could perhaps make an allegorical connection between the infestation of the baobabs and the rise of Nazism in Europe, but that would be too temporal a reference to fit the universality of the fairy tale. There is no personal animosity directed toward the baobabs; they are what they are. On Earth they fit naturally into the landscape, but on asteroid B-612, they are an environmental disaster.

In considering matters of consequence Saint-Exupéry fuses the good with the true in order to avoid at all costs the hypocrisy of uncommitted rationalism. Likewise, he fuses the bad with the false, as he does in *The Little Prince*, to emphasize that no matter how difficult it may be, when it comes to action, both of them are to be avoided or obliterated, no matter what the cost. In his letters and other writings Saint-Exupéry often used trees metaphorically to express his acceptance of the relativity of truth. One such example is in *Wind, Sand and Stars*:

> Truth is not that which can be demonstrated by the aid of logic. If
> orange-trees are hardy and rich in fruit in this bit of soil and not

that, then this bit of soil is what is truth for orange-trees. If a particular religion, or culture, or scale of values, if one form of activity rather than another, brings self-fulfillment to a man, releases the prince asleep within him unknown to himself, then that scale of values, that culture, that form of activity, constitute truth. Logic, you say? Let logic wangle its own explanation of life. (*WSS*, 240–41)

The pilot himself is most proud of his full-page illustration of the baobab tree, demonstrating that if but one of them were left to grow it would engulf the little prince's entire planet. This indeed would have been the result if the boy had failed in his duty. As the pilot points out, he has worked with extra diligence on this particular drawing because he wants it to cry out: "Children . . . watch out for the baobabs!" (22).

THE STARS

The sky and all that one finds in it are also a part of the landscape. The horizon, where land and sky meet, has always been the goal to which navigators set their charts, and metaphorically it's the point of destiny, the place toward which one will travel to see what lies beyond. Of course, the sky at night is another matter. When night falls it obliterates the horizon; it casts a luminous blanket over the landscape and everything takes on a new appearance. Substance and shadow unite. At night the word *heavens* becomes an appropriate substitute for *sky*. One's eyes lift naturally to survey the wonder of the night sky—a wonder that the great modern advances of science and technology have not diminished.

In poetry and story the stars have always been a powerfully evocative source. One of the first poems children learn gives them the opportunity to speak directly to any one of these sparkling marvels of the night sky:

> Twinkle, twinkle little star
> How I wonder what you are, . . .

They serve early on as magical charms as well:

> Starlight, star bright
> First star I see tonight
> I wish I may, I wish I might
> Get the wish I wish tonight.

Stars play an important role in all of Saint-Exupéry's writing, as his earlier titles indicate. In *Night Flight* the pilot-navigators rely on the stars to help them arrive safely at their destination. More important for the writer, however, they are touchstones of metaphor, amulets of wonder, helping him to alleviate his loneliness by carrying his thoughts to other places and other times, peopled by those he loves. Sometimes, Saint-Exupéry points out, the stars are themselves navigators—each showing a true direction, each a star of Bethlehem serving its own god: "This one points to a far-off well that is difficult to reach. . . . Another star guides you to an unknown oasis that the nomads sing of, . . . another star points to one of the white cities of the south. . . .Finally . . . from a great distance: a childhood home vividly remembered, a friend one knows nothing of, except that he exists" (*WW*, 108–9).

Stars add a great deal to the evocative power of *The Little Prince* as well. They contribute to the feeling of melancholia and otherworldliness that hangs over the story, which unobtrusively draws the reader from outside the confines of the story to the inside of all that is taking place. One hardly notices, but in the illustrations stars are sprinkled throughout the book. They appear on the cover, front, and back, on the title page and in more than one-third of the pictures accompanying the text. Stars appear even on the epaulets of the little prince's royal coat (11).

It is the stars that keep the memory of the little boy alive in the heart of the pilot. Years after their encounter in the desert, the aviator loves "to listen to the stars. It is like five hundred little bells" (89). Concentrating on the stars allows the drama to continue for him, though it takes place light-years away, on the tiny planet to which the little prince has returned. The fate of the flower is still of great consequence to him, because it is of great consequence to the little boy he has come to love.

More than once, by singling out one star from among the millions in the heavens, Saint-Exupéry emphasizes the importance of singularity. No matter how small and seemingly insignificant something or somebody may be, simply being loved grants it great consequence. For the boy, it is the rose he has left behind that singles his star out from all the others. When he is preparing to leave the earth, with the help of the snake, he comforts the aviator who has become his friend. He says: "I cannot show you where my star is to be found. It is better like that. My star will be just one of the stars for you. And so you will love to watch all the stars in the heavens . . . They will all be your friends" (85). For Saint-Exupéry the secret to loving everyone is to be uncovered by truly loving someone.

In the very last sentence of his story, the aviator directly addresses those who, like himself, possess childlike vision, for "no grown-up will ever understand that this is a matter of so much importance!" He entreats them to "Look up at the sky. Ask yourselves: Is it yes or no? Has the sheep eaten the flower? And you will see how everything changes" (91).

The final illustration of the story shows the little prince's final moment on earth. Atop the sand dune that is the appointed place for his final meeting with the snake, he is falling "gently as a tree falls" (90). Directly above him is his star, the one to which he must return in order to be once again with his beloved rose.

Immediately following is an unpaged epilogue accompanied by a very simple illustration. It is a repetition of the picture on page 90, but without the little prince—just two curved intersecting lines of the desert dunes with the lone star directly above. In the epilogue the pilot speaks directly to his readers, drawing them into the drama that mysteriously continues out there in star-filled space, beyond the pages of the book. Imploringly he urges others to help him never to forget. He says in part: "This is, to me, the loveliest and saddest landscape in the world. It is the same as that on the preceding page, but I have drawn it again to impress it on your memory. It is here that the little prince appeared on Earth, and disappeared."

THE FOX

The most excerpted portion of *The Little Prince* is the conversation he has with a fox. I once assumed that the author had taken the option permitted by the fairy tale form and placed a storybook fox—from an Aesop fable, perhaps—into a desert environment to which the species is not indigenous. So much for my knowledge of the Sahara. Not only do foxes live there, but Saint-Exupéry came to be intimate with one during the crash experience described in *Wind, Sand and Stars*. I say intimate even though he never saw the fox, or any fox for that matter.

In his search for water, he came upon the hole of a fennec, a long-eared carnivorous sand-fox the size of a rabbit (the type of fox accurately illustrated by Saint-Exupéry in *The Little Prince*.) Although he never saw the animal, he followed its tracks, hoping it would lead him to water. Imagining the fox's actions and motivations, he soon found himself using the possessive pronoun, referring to it as "my little fox." The tracks finally led back to the hole in which "he" (the fox) lives. Imagining the fennec crouched below, listening to his footsteps, Saint-Exupéry actually addressed him aloud, "Fox, my little fox" (*WSS*, 209).

In this dramatic search for water that is essential for physical survival, Saint-Exupéry has become surprisingly aware of a spiritual thirst that must be satisfied as well. The little fox that never appears helps him first to recognize the longing for friendship that lies unnoticed in the secret recesses of his heart, and then by its imagined presence assists him in finding relief for this spiritual thirst, which is magnified by the desolation and aloneness of the Sahara. In *The Little Prince*, however, this little fox becomes more than a silent presence: He comes on stage. The genre of the fairy tale gives him animation and voice. He speaks openly of secrets.

One of the secrets the fox teaches the little prince is the secret of "taming": something to which men have paid little attention. When the boy asks him what the word means and why it is important, the fox replies: "To me, you are still nothing more than a little boy who is just like a hundred thousand other little boys. And I have no need of you. And you, on your part, have no need of me. To you, I am nothing more than a fox like a hundred thousand other foxes. But if you tame me, you will be unique in all the world. To you, I shall be unique in all the world" (66).

And when they are parting the fox once again reminds him: "You become responsible, forever, for what you have tamed" (71).

In *Wisdom of the Sands*, Saint-Exupéry's posthumously published philosophical work, the responsibility of love in the "taming" process is put forth in much the same way as in *The Little Prince*. In one of the anecdotes, he tells of a desert man who snared a sand-fox cub, young enough for him to teach it to eat from his hand. Every day the little fox would grow more precious to him. He would delight in its silky fur and playful ways, but above all in its need for food, which made it depend on him for so much care and solicitude. In the simplicity of his heart he hugged the illusion that he was imparting something of himself to the little creature—that it was nourished and molded by his love. When the little fox was killed by a predator, the friends of the man suggested that he should catch and tame another. No. "Too much patience is needed—not for the catching, but for loving it" (*WS*, 47).

The fox in *The Little Prince* is a fine teacher, for like all creatures of barren places, he has suffered the pangs of extreme thirst. He recognizes immediately that the little boy's thirst is for companionship. In their first encounter the little prince says that he is "looking for friends" (66). And so the fox designs his lesson on friendship, including the caution to the boy that he may not find friendship among men as he assumes, since men now "buy things all ready made at the shops. But there is no shop anywhere where one can buy friendship and so men have no friends anymore" (67).

Saint-Exupéry experienced himself the intense thirst for companionship, so he has no trouble in giving these words to the fox. In the fall of 1940, in Portugal and hoping to find his way to the United States, he was truly on the edge of despair. Almost none of his flying companions were left. Then on 27 November, he received word that his good friend Captain Guillaumet was dead, his plane having been shot down over the Mediterranean. His anguish and sense of loss cries out in a letter dated 1 December 1940:

> Guillaumet is dead and tonight I feel I have no friends left.
> I have not a single comrade left to whom I can say: "Do you remember?" What a perfect desert. . . .
> The whole of life has to be begun again. Try to help me see the landscape, I beg of you. I'm in despair of being on the downward slope.
> Tell me what to do. (*WW*, 53–54)

The other secrets that the fox shares with the little prince are the thematic core of the story and will be taken up in more depth in the chapters that follow.

THE GARDEN

The little prince, after walking a long time through sand and rocks, suddenly is standing before a garden full of blooming roses (62), thousands that all look exactly like the flower he thought to be the only one in existence. Not yet having met the fox and benefited from his insightfulness, the boy is overcome with sadness: "And he lay down in the grass and cried" (64). The garden is used, much like the stars, to illuminate the difficulty one has in recognizing the uniqueness of one object of nature from all others of the same kind. The difficulty stems from the fact that the uniqueness arises not from a matter of appearance, but from an invisible secret between the subject and the object itself—a responsibility we must assume for the things we call our own.

The boy prince has not yet realized that he has already had a garden of his own, even though it consisted of but one rose. More important, he has not yet recognized that he has been in every sense of the word a responsible gardener. In contrast to the businessman and other grown-ups like him, the prince has not submitted the things of nature to his own selfish whims. He has faithfully cared for everything on his planet—tending his flower, cleaning out his volcanoes (32).

In a fairy tale one need not question the existence of a rose garden in the middle of a desert. In fact, the metaphor is stronger because of it. Where else but in the contrasting desolation of the desert could a garden of blossoming roses possess such symbolic power? For the ancient people of the desert lands the garden always carried deep spiritual significance—so much so that the Greeks borrowed the Persian word for *garden* to denote paradise in their own language.

It is not surprising that the garden turns up in *The Little Prince*, because Saint-Exupéry's other works are filled with garden references. In a letter written only a few months before his death, he describes his lifelong desire for peace—that someday he hopes not to be completely at rest, but at least serenely in tune with nature and the natural course of events. He writes:

> I've always divided human beings into two categories: those who resemble a courtyard and suffocate you between their walls—
> Then there are those who resemble a garden, where you can walk and be silent, and breathe. (*WW*, 200)

In his final writings, the garden emerges as the culminating symbol for his life and thought, because at the center of the garden stands the gardener—the one who cares for the flowers, the trees, and the shrubs. At the very end of *Wisdom of the Sands* we find Saint-Exupéry's parting message to the world:

> I enter into communion with all gardeners, living and dead, through the only channel that conveys such messages, the way of words that well up silently from the heart: *this morning I, too, have pruned my rose trees.* Little matters if the message pursues its silent way for many years, or in the end reaches this man or that. So as to enter into communion with my gardeners I have taken the simplest course; I have done homage to their god, which is a rose tree glimmering in the dusk of dawn. (*WS*, 349)

If perchance we forget Saint-Exupéry's sobering words concerning our responsibility to the world in which we find ourselves, we have other people to remind us: Albert Schweitzer, Chief Seattle, Martin

Buber, and Rachel Carson to name but a few. Remember, too, the last sentence of Voltaire's *Candide*, a tale that resembles *The Little Prince* in many ways: " ' 'Tis well said,' replied Candide, 'but we must cultivate our gardens.' "[3]

THE ROSE

This talk of gardens, of course, leads us to the rose. There is so much to be said about the love affair between the little prince and his tiny flower that it will take up most of the next two chapters. For Saint-Exupéry himself, this is the center of his tale, the object of his own affection. Here is the all important *each* within the *all*—the "one small boy and not another" in *Wisdom of the Sands*, the one sheep for whom the good shepherd painstakingly searches, the victim of highway rogues for whom the Samaritan interrupts his journey, the prodigal son. In his own life it is his mother, his sister, his friend Léon Werth, a small girl on a French farm—each one somewhere on the other side of the Atlantic.

Each time I read from *The Little Prince* I am drawn to a room of a house on Eaton's Neck in Northport, Long Island, only a short distance from my home. And there in the late night or early morning hours, when he did his writing, I see the writer himself choked with sadness. The year is 1941 and these loved ones are all living in Nazi-occupied France. Like ghosts, they haunt his dream of consciousness and make all of his travails and sacrifices not only worthwhile, but perhaps necessary. This is metaphor in its most animistic form. It is shaped out of the anguish of the heart, not the cleverness of the intellect.

It is on the fifth day after the accident that "the secret of the little prince's life was revealed to me" (25). When the boy continues his relentless questioning concerning the eating habits of sheep, the aviator tells him that a sheep "eats anything it finds in its reach" (26). This piece of information upsets the boy, because he realizes that by bringing a sheep to his asteroid in order to introduce a more efficient means for destroying the baobabs, he would at the same time place the one

flower growing there in great peril. The pilot, who is concentrating on
unscrewing a bolt that got stuck in the engine, thoughtlessly dismisses
the boy's concern.

> "Don't you see—I am very busy with matters of consequence!"
> He stared at me thunderstruck.
> "Matters of consequence!"
> "You talk just like the grown-ups!. . . "
> "You mix everything up together . . . "
> "I know a planet where there is a certain red-faced gentleman.
> He has never smelled a flower. He has never looked at a star. He
> has never loved any one. . . . And all day he says over and over,
> just like you: 'I am busy with matters of consequence!'. . . he is
> not a man—he is a mushroom!"
> "A what?"
> "A mushroom!"
> The little prince was now white with rage! (26–27)

As the proliferation of exclamation marks indicates, this is no
longer a conversation, but a high-pitched argument wherein strong
beliefs are at stake. His words choked with sobbing, the little prince
concludes his position by exclaiming: "If some one loves a flower, of
which just one single blossom grows in all the millions and millions of
stars. . . . you think that is not important!" (27–28). So agitated is he
at this point that the exclamation mark overwhelmingly deletes the
implied question mark altogether.

The aviator soon comes to know the prince's flower better. She
arrived on the tiny planet as a seed blown from no one knew where.
The little prince gave the plant close attention once it began to grow,
since it did not resemble any of the small sprouts already there. When
the first bud appeared he felt "at once that some miraculous apparition
must merge from it" (29). Mesmerized by the rose's beauty, he nevertheless found it difficult to deal with her vanity. He was quick to recognize the absurdity of her statements, such as her claim that she was
not at all afraid of tigers. Having for some time taken seriously her
words that were in truth without importance, he became unhappy
with himself.

Now in retrospect, telling his story to the pilot, he understands the error in his behavior toward this fragile and naive flower. He realizes that it was a mistake to listen to her: One ought never to listen to flowers, but simply to look at them and breathe in their fragrance. He says: "The fact is that I did not know how to understand anything! I ought to have judged by deeds and not by words. She cast her fragrance and her radiance over me. I ought never to have run away from her" (32).

At this point in the narrative both the aviator and the reader might surmise that the little prince has come by this new insight all by himself, but that is not the case. In the time within the story itself, though he has not yet revealed it, he has already completed his visits to other planets. Once upon Earth he has already met with the snake for the first time. Most important, he has had his conversations with the fox, who has given him wise counsel. All of this will be revealed later on, as his story unfolds. Nevertheless it is here in the early pages of the book that, for the reader, there is a foreshadowing of his growing need to return to his planet and his flower, and with it a growing suspicion of how difficult and perilous that journey might be.

All of Saint-Exupéry's writing, I think, merits the attention of today's reader. Many critics have rightfully said, sometimes to their own surprise, that *The Little Prince* is and will be his most lasting work. There should be no surprise about such a claim: this is clearly Saint-Exupéry's most mature work. It speaks powerfully to an audience outside his own time, chiefly because it uses the etiologic symbols provided by nature. It steps outside of political and historical time. It has all the marks of the good fairy tale—the higher or more complete kind, as described by J. R. R. Tolkien: it gives "to child or man that hears it, when the 'turn' comes, a catch of the breath, a beat and lifting of the heart near to (or indeed accompanied by) tears, as keen as that given by any form of literary art, and having a peculiar quality."[4]

6

Spirit: Silent and Invisible

After his encounter with the snake, the little prince comes suddenly upon the garden and its thousands of blooming roses.

> "Who are you?" he demanded thunderstruck.
> "We are roses," the roses said.
> And he was overcome with sadness. His flower had told him that she was the only one of her kind in all the universe. And here were five thousand of them, all alike, in one single garden! . . .
> And he lay down in the grass and cried. (62–64)

It is then that the fox appears, and in the next few pages the tenor of the story takes a dramatic shift. Indeed, the basic theme that Saint-Exupéry had already fashioned in a myriad of ways in his previous writings suddenly emerges in the unique simplicity and clarity of the fairy-tale form. Bits and phrases from these few pages are the most remembered and quoted pieces from all of his works. The fox is like the actor who has but a few moments on stage, but whose cameo appearance remains indelibly sketched in the memory of the audience.

Before they say goodbye the fox leaves the little prince with two very simple secrets in life, the first of which is: "It is only with the heart that one can see rightly; what is essential is invisible to the eye" (70).

To understand the full impact of this statement to Saint-Exupéry, one must attend to his other writings, as well. In June 1943, in one of the many long unmailed letters that may be interpreted as letters to himself, Saint-Exupéry writes not of the Sahara, but of the "terrible human desert" in which he finds himself. He expresses a profound personal sadness as well as a pity for his generation, which "lacks all human substance. Having known no spiritual values . . . the sickness does not lie in any absence of individual talent, but in the way people are forbidden, under pain of ridicule, to turn to the great refreshing myths. . . . There is one problem and only one in the world: to revive in people some sense of spiritual meaning" (*WW*, 133–34).

He prophetically sends forth the alarm to the peoples of the world that while they are physically coming closer to one another through the astounding advances of technology, the essential community of the spirit—Augustine's *City of God*—is withering away, speeding toward oblivion. He is reluctant to make propaganda speeches on the radio because "it is indecent when you have no bible to offer people" (*WW*, 28). His writing, though addressed to others, is above all written for himself. It is the continuous process of trying to better himself, in spirit, through exercise and testing. He writes:

> My teeth, my liver, and the rest are moldering away and my body is of no intrinsic interest. I want to be something different when it is time to die.
>
> Perhaps all this [writing] is trivial. . . . I don't care. It is the best I can become. I must become better—. (*WW*, 69)

In a less personal vein, he writes: "Civilization is an invisible tie, because it has not to do with things but with the invisible ties that join one thing to another in a particular way" (*WW*, 137).

Following the fall of France and his fateful flight over Arras, Saint-Exupéry began to compose *Letter to a Hostage*. He felt compelled to send a message of hope and love to those he had left behind, assuring them that they would not be forgotten, that they indeed were the true heroes of the historical drama that was unfolding. At the same time, the seeds of *The Little Prince* were beginning to stir within his imagination. The ideas that he would so eloquently express expositorily in *Letter*, would soon surface again in a new and more powerful guise: the nondiscursive language and the fanciful form of the fairytale. Whereas expository prose is called forth, the true fairy tale comes into existence unobtrusively and unbidden.

The connection is made most clear in a segment of *Letter to a Hostage* in which he ruminates on the desert and the stars, seeing them as a fitting landscape for his inner cosmic journey. The stars now "are all stars of Bethlehem," each pointing a way; and the sand of the desert "is a fairy tale lawn. . . . Since the desert has no tangible riches, nothing to see or hear, and since the inner life, far from diminishing, flourishes there, one is forced to conclude that man is motivated first and foremost by invisible attractions. Man is ruled by the spiritual" (*WW*, 109).

This indeed is the stuff of which fairy tales are made.

I beg the reader's indulgence a bit more before I return to the text of *The Little Prince*. My reason for staying a bit longer with Saint-Exupéry's other writing is that certain passages reveal quite clearly the continuous struggle he had in shaping a written language for the duality of experience—for encounters with the outside world and within himself. That in the end he was still searching for more satisfactory words does not diminish the fact that in *The Little Prince* he had found words appropriate for 'a once upon a time' story, one that transcended in meaning and impact the confines of his immediate time and place.

This double life he lived and expressed is perhaps Saint-Exupéry's most identifiable quality. It is not unique; all of the great writers go through life with their feet firmly planted on solid earth, while their imaginations wander in more ethereal realms. They are at their best when it comes to posing the basic questions of existence that so many of us evade, except perhaps when experiencing personal moments of anguish or great exhilaration. They are always reaching beyond words to snare, if only partially, the reality of the spirit. Discussing this problem of the literary artist, Saint-Exupéry says:

expression is a slow, elusive task, and it is a mistake to assume that anything incapable of being stated in words does not exist. Stating is, by the same token, comprehending. But small indeed is the part of man which I have learned, so far, to comprehend. Yet that which on a certain day I come to comprehend existed none the less the day before; and foolish indeed were I to deem that all in man for which I cannot find the words is unworthy of consideration. (WS, 107)

In *Letter to a Hostage* Saint-Exupéry captures the magic of a single moment shared between two friends, himself and Léon Werth, as well as any essayist might, and yet he himself is aware that there must be a better way. Perhaps the best way is through silence—an art without words—but he is a writer after all, so he will instinctively continue to look for a better way.

> We were completely at peace, sheltered from disorder by a perennial civilization. We tasted a kind of bliss. . . . We felt pure, righteous, luminous, and indulgent. We could not have expressed what profound truth was revealed to us, but we felt absolute certainty—an almost overweening certainty.
> The universe was showing its goodwill through us. (WW, 111)
> [It] is very difficult to explain. I am in danger of capturing merely the reflections, not the essence. (WW, 112)

He follows this with a little story from one of his experiences during the Spanish civil war, in which he attempts to demonstrate that very often that which is essential is weightless—in this case it is a smile, a smile that "can make you die for it" (WW, 112). In *The Little Prince* the laughter of the little boy has about it the same transmission of essence.

The myth for him is the common measure around which a people can draw together their different qualities. The pursuit of political correctness is not enough; the varied theses that are put forth must be made around a common transcendental image. It is in contemplating this issue that he recognizes a distinction between intelligence and spirit: "Spirit indicates the direction, the spiritual point of view—the choice of star" (*WW*, 144). Here again, while using the discursive language of the epistle, he admits the limitations of clarity: "I am not expressing myself clearly, although I know precisely what I'm trying to say" (*WW*, 145).

While World War II was going on, and as he looked forward to its aftermath, he would not divide Frenchmen politically, by their choice of a leader—de Gaulle, Giraud, Petain—but rather by the spiritual ideal that dominated their thinking, by their choice of a star. "My brothers are those who have loved as I have, not reasoned as I have—and I use the word 'love' in its initial sense of 'spiritual contemplation'" (*WW*, 145).

Here we have an example of the artist's mind at work. He does not negate intelligence. His work doesn't arise out of raw passion alone, but out of a blend of intelligence and feeling that carries him into a deeper realm of thought than most pundits dare to enter. He does not dichotomize intelligence and spirit, but rather recognizes that in all matters of consequence intelligence cannot be separated from will, and that the "choice of star" is in the end what will determine the goodness or evil of an action.

Just as intelligence cannot be isolated, neither can emotion; they must work in concert. In another unmailed letter he writes: "To my way of thinking, passion is a blind monster— . . . the Spirit walks on human feet. Then it is blind and it devastates. It turns into emotion on the lower level" (*WW*, 161). Always he is reaching for the transcendental particular that will intrinsically balance thought and feeling so that moral responsibility becomes a harmonious and inevitable consequence. So many thinkers do not take their ponderings beyond the point where they realize that the net result will in all probability be personal pain and sacrifice. One could say of Saint-Exupéry something very like what T.S. Eliot says of Blake: that he possessed "a peculiar honesty, which in a world too frightened to be honest, is peculiarly terrifying. It is an honesty against which the whole world conspires, because it is unpleasant. . . . There was . . . nothing to distract him from his interests or to corrupt those interests. . . . These circumstances . . . are what make him innocent."[1]

The trepidations Saint-Exupéry had concerning democracy did not rise from ideology, but rather from his personal experience and observations of the behavior of those people who live in the democracies of the world. He had a great detestation of the mob, large groups with special interests, or others blindly following some cause or leader.

He sensually associates the mob with frenetic movement and noise, an environment in which the individual will find it difficult to survive. When he writes the following in *Wisdom of the Sands*, I think he is writing about his own sense of frustration during his last years: "a people that forbids one of its number to break free from the herd and isolate himself on the mountaintop—surely they are murderers of the spirit. For the domain of the spirit, where it can spread its wings, is—silence" (*WS*, 93).

Partner to invisibility is silence, and that too is implicitly included in the first secret shared by the fox. In the meager language of physical and mortal humanity, these words are almost always presented as absences, because the ordinary use of the senses gives only limited evidence of their existence. Neither does the power of reason give one much help in grasping their living presence. The counting process and the naming process, both so predominant in early schooling, are the foundation for a system of thought that is bound by perceptual time and space. In contrast, invisibility and silence, like myth and eternity, exist beyond space and time, and thus ordinary language and thought are inadequate to describe the essence of spirit.

The dictionary itself defines silence as "an absence." The usual way for most people to deal with an absence is not to deal with it at all. For children, silence is difficult, and more often than not they are commanded into silence rather than shown ways to enter into it. Therefore, they come to believe that to be silent means to do nothing, and this belief makes it difficult for most of them to successfully create imaginative silence. But in his writing, Saint-Exupéry shares with readers, both young and old, the sudden unexpected dreams that come to him in silence, when he is awake or asleep, or most often when he is in a state suspended between both. The odors, smells, and sounds of memory rise slowly out of the silence. He continually searches "to find a meaning in this silence made of a thousand silences" (*WSS*, 107). In *The Little Prince*, as in his other works, he presents spirit, compositionally invisible and silent, as an ethereal reality, a presence, a something—not an absence, or a negative of something else.

An incident near the end of the story contains a bit of irony that might easily be passed over, because by this time the reader is caught up in the fate of the little prince. He meets a merchant who is selling pills, one of which taken weekly will completely quench one's thirst. When asked about the usefulness of these pills, the merchant points out that computations by experts show that they will save 53 minutes of every week.

> "And what do I do with these fifty-three minutes?"
> "Anything you like . . ."
> "As for me," said the little prince to himself, "if I had fifty-three minutes to spend as I liked, I should walk at my leisure toward a spring of fresh water." (74)

Time and space are man-made concepts, though they are too often thought of as substantive entities. Seconds, minutes, hours, days, months, years, centuries, ages, eons—computations that seemingly draw one closer to the eternal, when in fact it is all a man-made mirage of self-delusion. The fairy tale, on the other hand, requires us to consider timelessness. As Tolkien says: "one can scarcely improve on the formula *Once upon a time*. It has an immediate effect. . . . It produces at a stroke the sense of a great unchartered world of time."[2]

In one segment of *Letter to a Hostage* Saint-Exupéry poses several questions for himself:

> How does life build the vital currents that we live from? Where does the magnetic force that pulls me towards this friends' house originate? What are the essential moments that made this presence into a vital pole for me? What are the secret events that mold particular affections, and through them, love of country?
>
> How little stir the real miracles cause! How simple are the most vital events! (*WW*, 110)

Simple, perhaps, but not so simple to explain, not so simple that they can be answered by exposition. Such questions are uncovered and illuminated best through the nondiscursive language of poetry and story. Here, that which best responds to the question mark is not the reasoned and horizontally planed period, but rather the wonder-filled and shimmering mark of exclamation. In fairy tales, miracles need no explanation because they are common events.

When they first meet, the little prince implores the fox, whom he finds "very pretty to look at," to come play with him, since he is so unhappy. The fox tells him that first the boy must "tame" him, to which the boy replies:

"What does that mean—'tame'?"
"It is an act too often neglected," said the fox. "It means to establish ties."
"'To establish ties'?"
"Just that," said the fox. "To me, you are still nothing more than a little boy who is just like a hundred thousand other little boys. And I have no need of you. And you, on your part, have no need of me. To you, I am nothing more than a fox like a hundred thousand other foxes. But if you tame me, then we shall need each other. To me, you will be unique in all the world. To you, I shall be unique in all the world . . ."
"I am beginning to understand," said the little prince. "There is a flower . . . I think that she has tamed me." (66)

There it is—encompassed in a brief paragraph: the secret of see-ing with the heart. It can be done only by focusing on an "each" with-in the "all."

In the meditation numbered 110 in *Wisdom of the Sands*, Saint-Exupéry uses a poignant parable to illustrate the unique power that accompanies seeing with the heart. In it the ministers of the ruling prince report to him concerning a disaster in his realm in which the lives of several children were lost. He admonishes them for couching their report in the language of statistics, placing the importance on the numbers of victims. He says:

[S]uch arithmetic means nothing to me; . . . since the beginning of
the empire, children have died by hundreds of thousands . . .

I shall be moved to tears if you can take me to an individual
child, by a path leading to him alone, and (even as a single flower
brings home to us all flowers), by way of him, I shall feel for all
children, and weep not only for the children, but for suffering
mankind. (*WS*, 299–300)

Notice, if you will, the parenthetical reference to the single
flower. Here, as in the fox's secret-sharing, Saint-Exupéry illustrates the
important difference between reporting and storytelling. The first is
done through the eyes of the intellect: surveying broad panoramas,
gathering essential facts, avoiding any expression of feeling that might
blur or distort the objectivity of the account. It is the "seeing" method
used by journalists, historians, economists, and government officials. It
is often, in modern parlance, an attempt to get at the "big picture." The
eyes of the heart, on the other hand, purposely zero in on each of the
individual dramas that may be playing out within the broader arena.

The fox then shares the reason for his great desire to be tamed by
the little boy: "it will be as if the sun came to shine on my life. . . . You
have hair that is the color of gold. . . . The grain, which is also golden,
will bring me back the thought of you. And I shall love to listen to the
wind in the wheat" (67).

We have in the fox a very able teacher. After giving the reason
for the importance of taming, he gazes at the little prince for a long
time, before impassionately pleading: "Please—tame me!" And when
the boy tells him he has important matters to attend to—"friends to
discover, and a great many things to understand"—the fox is ready
with his rebuttal. "One only understands the things one tames. . . .
Men have no more time to understand anything. They buy things
already made at the shops. But there is no shop anywhere where one
can buy friendship, and so men have no friends any more. If you want
a friend, tame me" (67).

The little prince is now fully motivated, and he eagerly places
himself in the hands of the teacher, asking: "What must I do to tame
you?" And the lessons begin.

The first lesson concerns the one behavioral virtue of which young children are most in need—and they will most often laughingly agree with you when you point it out to them: patience. This taming process takes time (like the awakening of the seed). It begins by sitting quietly at a distance from one another and then coming closer each day. The fox emphasizes the need for silence: "you will say nothing. Words are the source of misunderstandings" (67).

When the boy returns the next day the fox tells him it would have been better had he come back at the same hour as their previous encounter. If he, the fox, knew when his 'tamer' was to return he should begin to feel happier an hour earlier, and continue to feel happier and happier. And by the time the meeting occurs he "shall already be worrying and jumping about." He emphasizes that proper rites must be observed. When his student asks, "What is a rite?," he replies, as a good teacher will, not only with a concise definition, but with an example of clarity:

> [Rites are] actions too often neglected, . . . they are what make one day different from other days, one hour from other hours. There is a rite, for example, among my hunters. Every Thursday they dance with the village girls. So Thursday is a wonderful day for me! I can take a walk as far as the vineyards. But if the hunters danced at just any time, every day would be like every other day, and I should never have any vacation at all. (68)

The importance of ritual in the education of the young is a topic I will return to in the appendix. For now let me just emphasize that in today's schools ritual is indeed, in the words of the fox, an act "too often neglected." It is through ritual, freshly conceived and carried out, that one transforms the everyday, the obvious, the seemingly insignificant, the sometimes forgotten, and probes through the surface of familiarity in search of some invisible composition, some secret seed of the heart, that may be waiting to be brought to bloom. Ritual is an essential component of celebration, and one can never learn to celebrate through rote. Take the spirit out of the ritual and the saluting of the flag, the planting of a tree on Earth Day, or even the blowing out of candles on a birthday cake have little significance at all. Each act becomes more of a chore than a celebration. There is no hallelujah; that comes only when the heart is moved.

Having observed the proper rites of taming, the two come to love one another. And later, when it is time to part, the fox admits that he must cry. Then follows this brief exchange between the two:

> "It is your own fault," said the little prince. "I never wished you any sort of harm; but you wanted me to tame you . . ."
> "Yes, that is so," said the fox.
> "But now you are going to cry!" said the little prince.
> "Yes, that is so," said the fox.
> "Then it has done you no good at all!"
> "It has done me good," said the fox, "because of the color of the wheat fields." (68)

Once more we find a close relationship between the metaphoric substance of this fanciful story and a previous work of Saint-Exupéry's in which he describes, from both within and without, a dramatic and significant scene from his own experience. In *Flight to Arras*, he returns to his billet in a farmhouse just as the farmer, his wife, and his young niece are sitting down to supper. As the farmer silently breaks the bread and hands it round, Saint-Exupéry thinks of the farmer's wide fields of wheat, from which the substance of the bread has come. And because tomorrow the wheat fields, like the farmer and his family, may be gone because of the approaching army of the Third Reich, he conjures up a vision that traces the wheat from seed, to the making of the bread, to the final consumption of the bread by humans. As he says: "There is no savour like that of bread shared between men. And I saw of a sudden that the energy contained in this spiritual food, this bread of the spirit generated by that field of wheat, was in peril. Tomorrow, perhaps, . . . my farmer would not be celebrating this same household rite" (*FA*, 212–13).

His gaze then turns on the little girl who sits beside him, in whom the bread made from the wheat "is transmuted into languid grace" (*FA*, 213). And when she smiles at him, he murmurs to himself:

" 'The peace of the kingdom of silence.' That smile was the flow of the shining wheat" (*FA*, 217).

I have waited until now to include the symbolic significance of the wheat fields because it more appropriately belongs to the teaching ingenuity of the fox than to the landscape itself. Early on in his teaching the fox says to his pupil: "see the grain-fields down yonder? I do not eat bread. Wheat is of no use to me. The wheat fields have nothing to say to me. And that is sad. But you have hair that is the color of gold. Think how wonderful that will be when you have tamed me! The grain, which is golden, will bring me back the thought of you. And I shall love to listen to the wind in the wheat" (67).

One yearns never to forget those whom one has come to love, even if that love is the result of a single brief encounter. For if love is not, as the poet says, eternal, we still wish it to be. The world of nature is filled with sensual reminders that help to keep love alive in the halls of memory, even after the loved one is no longer physically present. It is the golden color of the wheat that will forever remind the fox of the prince; it is the smell of the lilacs each spring that in Walt Whitman's elegiac poem forever reminds him of the beloved Abraham Lincoln.[3] And for Saint-Exupéry the sight of wheat fields would always conjure up that one brief mystical moment when he shared a smile with a little girl in war-torn France.

The importance of *The Little Prince* as a piece of literature, especially in regard to its effect on the reader, depends upon the degree of importance given to the words of the fox. Taken euphemistically, the message imparts little more than an entreaty for kindness, and the symbol of the heart carries with it little more power than the one commonly displayed on valentine cards. Taken literally, however, the words of the fox raise some very basic and profound questions. Who am I? What is life all about? Are there truths to be found through faith and feeling as well as through empirical investigation?

In *The Little Prince* the heart is no euphemism, but rather a symbol of the spiritual depths of each individual. Saint-Exupéry finds the spiritual world of adulthood to be impoverished, in a state of famine, mainly because adults have forgotten or ignored the fact that the heart is the invisible bond that brings men together and enables them to embrace the natural world in which they find themselves. In a world of material abundance, he finds spiritual poverty. Love, for him, is not a matter of choice but one of necessity. It is a matter of consequence—indeed, a matter of survival. Humans must learn to love one another, as well as all creation, or perish.

The little prince learns his lessons well in the classroom of the fox. At one point later in the story he and the pilot exchange observations:

> "The men where you live," said the little prince, "raise five thousand roses in the same garden—and they do not find in it what they are looking for."
>
> "They do not find it," I replied.
>
> "And yet what they are looking for could be found in one single rose or in a little water."
>
> "Yes, that is true," I said.
>
> And the little prince added: "But the eyes are blind. One must look with the heart." (79)

It has taken the pilot some time to tune in to the meanings expressed by the boy. During much of the early conversations he has listened without comment because he realizes "that it was impossible to cross-examine him." Near the conclusion of the story, however, when they are speaking of beauty and the prince remarks that the desert is beautiful, the aviator suddenly realizes that the little boy has been saying things that he has known all his life, though they have rarely caught his attention. He muses: "And that was true. I have always loved the desert. One sits down on a desert sand dune, sees nothing, hears nothing. Yet through the silence something throbs, and gleams" (75).

And when the little prince adds that what also makes the desert beautiful is that somewhere it hides a well, the aviator is astonished by his sudden understanding of the radiance of the desert sands. And with this understanding comes the further realization that much of what the boy has been saying all along, especially those things he learned from the fox, is true: that which is essential, which gives things their beauty "is something that is invisible" (76).

This revelation also brings a new dimension to their relationship. The pilot now realizes that the little prince has become for him what the flower is for the boy himself. The following passage deftly describes how suddenly one becomes aware of falling in love, and also of why it has happened.

> As the little prince dropped off to sleep, I took him in my arms and set out walking once more. I felt deeply moved, and stirred. It seemed to me that I was carrying a very fragile treasure. It seemed to me, even, that there was nothing more fragile on all the Earth. In the moonlight I looked at his pale forehead, his closed eyes, his locks of hair that trembled in the wind, and I said to myself: "What I see here is nothing but a shell. What is most important is invisible . . ."
> As his lips opened slightly with the suspicion of a half-smile, I said to myself, again: "What moves me so deeply, about this little prince who is sleeping here, is his loyalty to a flower—the image of a rose that shines through his whole being like a flame of a lamp, even when he is asleep . . ." And I felt him to be more fragile still. I felt the need of protecting him, as if he himself were a flame that might be extinguished by a little puff of wind. (76)

This fragile and ephemeral little being, who has dedicated his life to protecting one even more fragile and ephemeral than himself; has stolen the heart of this man of the world. The invisible flame of true charity silently passes through the one and into the heart of the other, giving it a light of new understanding. The pilot's life will be changed forever.

Saint-Exupéry, like Pascal, a man of exceptionally keen intelligence, first set forth to test his reason against the mysteries of the world around him, only to find that reason declares itself powerless to get beyond a partial and relative knowledge of the universe. He came to realize that for him the visible world was but an imperceptible dot in the vastness of the cosmos. He did not then discard reason as an avenue of investigation but rather infused it with a searching of the heart, which helps to illuminate man's limited power and his unlimited aspirations, his pettiness and his grandeur.

The little prince and his pilot friend do not unravel the mystery confronting them, but they do come to realize that the happiness they seek is wrapped up in the infinite mystery of existence. They begin to learn to see with their hearts, though when they speak it is with the calm assurance of the logician: "If some one loves a flower, of which first one single blossom grows in all the millions and millions of stars, it is enough to make him happy just to look at the stars. He can say to himself: Somewhere my flower is there" (27–28).

Saint-Exupéry is always using the language of things to point beyond things, to the ultimate invisible order. He reaches beyond appearance to grasp the essential spirit of things. Empirically, things *are*, or at least appear to be, but in the realm of the spirit things metaphorically *stand for*. Young readers of *The Little Prince* are brought in touch with those realities of the spirit which are not completely within their comprehension, but traces of which they find in their homes, their communities, their places of worship, as well as in their natural surroundings. They also receive within this slim volume a strong affirmation that the spiritual quest is not only universal, but worthwhile.

Through metaphor, Saint-Exupéry concretizes the intangible. Through the power of creative imagination, he takes his readers into the mysterious realms of the human spirit. The torch of empiricism is best left behind, because the light will only contort or blind one to the wonder and beauty that lie within. The readers, like the author—like the little boy and the aviator in the story—must feel around in the shadows, relying heavily upon instinct to point the way. The author offers no answers, only explorations; no assurances, only invitations; no detailed or dogmatic explanations, only impulses—whispers and hints of meaning; shared secrets.

The journey of the little prince is a quest in pursuit of the meaning of love. It is a spiritual journey filled with mystery. It springs more from the heart than from the mind, and it is the hearts of its readers that it hopes to reach. As a mystical expression of faith, it is less susceptible to any language outside its own metaphor. Indeed, it may evaporate if it is placed under the scrutinous eye of empiricism. To emphasize once again, however, this is not to say that it is contradictory to the rules of logic. One may have good reasons for falling in love, but one doesn't fall in love simply by having good reasons. When the intellect performs naturally, it does so in combination with intuition, and the net result is, as Karl Jaspers says, "the unity of movement of Reason and experience . . . so that Plato was able to conceive Eros and Knowledge as one."[4]

So after all, is that the secret, the simple cliché: Love is what makes the world go round? I think it is, at least in Saint-Exupéry's view of all true matters of consequence. Isn't it love, after all, that everyone seems to be looking for, with too few finding it, because they have failed to find the "each" among the "others"? One cannot find love by looking at a garden of five thousand roses, but only "in one single rose." The eyes can perceive the *all*, but that is but seeing. As George MacDonald puts it, "Seeing is not believing—it is only seeing."[5] The little boy prince merely says: "the eyes are blind. One must look with the heart" (79).

7

I Am Responsible

After the fox has revealed to the little prince the secret of the taming process, he tells him to go and look again at the garden of roses. As the prince stands before them, he demonstrates that he has learned his lesson well: "'You are not at all like my rose,' he said. 'As yet you are nothing. No one has tamed you, and you have tamed no one. You are like my fox when I first knew him. He was only a fox like a hundred thousand other foxes. But I have made him my friend, and now he is unique in all the world'" (70).

A simple revelation, to be sure—one that children can understand with little trouble at all. They have experienced it themselves, so they can weigh its validity without help from others. Most of them too have already come across it in other stories, as well. In *Charlotte's Web*,[1] for instance, the growing acquaintanceship of the young pig Wilbur and Charlotte the spider finally blossoms into friendship, and by the end of the story young readers see to what ends a true friend will go in protecting a friend once found.

The little prince continues to address the roses:

"You are beautiful, but you are empty," he went on. "One could not die for you. To be sure, an ordinary passerby would think that

81

my rose looked just like you—the rose that belongs to me. But in herself alone she is more important than all the hundreds of other roses: because it is she that I have watered; because it is she that I have put under the glass globe; because it is she that I have sheltered behind the screen; because it is for her that I have killed the caterpillars (except the two or three that we saved to become butterflies); because it is she that I have listened to, when she grumbled, or boasted or even sometimes when she said nothing. Because she is *my* rose." (70)

And so it is that the little prince has grasped the significance of himself. His life has purpose. He has discovered that all of his everyday, routine chores—which had heretofore seemed so unimportant that he had felt the need to travel great distances in search of more momentous encounters—were in fact the true matters of consequence. When he will return to the fox to say goodbye, he will be given the two secrets I've mentioned earlier, the first of which was discussed in the previous chapter. But he has already learned the significance of the second as well, for he has said to the roses: "One could not die for you."

"Goodbye," said the fox. "And now here is my secret, a very simple secret: It is only with the heart that one can see rightly; what is essential is invisible to the eye."

"What is essential is invisible to the eye," the little prince repeated, so that he would be sure to remember.

"It is the time you have wasted for your rose that makes your rose so important."

"It is the time I have wasted for my rose—" said the little prince, so that he would be sure to remember.

"Men have forgotten this truth," said the fox. "But you must not forget it. You become responsible, forever, for what you have tamed. You are responsible for your rose . . ."

"I am responsible for my rose," the little prince repeated, so that he would be sure to remember. (70–71)

This could almost be considered one of those good news/bad news messages, depending upon how one weighs the meaning of the word responsible. The fox's message is not simply for discussion; it demands action. *The Little Prince* is no escape-from-reality fairy tale, but one that strips away the artificial considerations of materialism, conformity, and convenience. It goes to the core of the matter, which resides in the realm of the spirit.

The little prince seeks, after all, that truth which we all seek deep in our hearts: the meaning of love. His journey, plus the secrets of the fox, lead him to a simple answer, but that simplicity doesn't lessen the answer's gravity or validity. The prince is not merely a cute figure conjured up through the sentimental process of personal reminiscence. It is his innocent eye that enables him to grasp simple truths, be they pleasant or not. And as we will see shortly, once the truth has been discovered, he is moved to action, knowing full well what lies before him. He is a tragic lover, aware of the great consequences of love once found, and he faces them squarely.

Once he repeats the words "I am responsible for my rose," he knows what he must do. The appearance of things has changed, and as a result, all of his actions take on new meaning. When addressing the roses he had listed all of the things he had done to protect his rose, but the fox has added one more: "It is the time you have wasted on your rose that makes your rose so important."

In the taming or loving process Saint-Exupéry focuses on the lover, not the object of his affection. "The one thing that matters is the effort" (WS, 141)—making efficiency irrelevant as an instrument of measurement. Wasted time is the invisible, essential time that ties the knot of faithfulness and duty to a loved one. When referring to modern civilization, which is bereft of these wasted moments, he uses terms like *anthill, herd, robots*. One such example: "Don't you understand that somewhere along the way we have gone astray? The human anthill is richer than ever before. We have more wealth and more leisure, and yet we lack something essential, which we find difficult to describe. We feel less human; somewhere we have lost our mysterious prerogatives" (WW, 4).

At another time he writes: "In this age of divorce, one divorces oneself just as easily from things. Refrigerators are interchangeable—and homes, too, if they represent nothing more than a bundle of habits—so also with a wife, a religion, or a political party. One cannot even be unfaithful: there is nothing to be unfaithful to" (*WW*, 36).

When he leaves the fox the little prince meets a watchman, and during their brief conversation Saint-Exupéry reemphasizes this point. " 'Only the children know what they are looking for,' said the little prince. 'They waste their time over a rag doll and it becomes very important to them; and if anybody takes it away from them, they cry'" (73).

Children's play is not frivolous escape. For children, playing is the most serious thing in the world. As Chesterton points out: "the man writing on motherhood is merely an educationalist; the child playing with a doll is a mother."[2] Those today who advocate more education for parenting should heed these words. Child's play is less an escape into nothingness than a retreat into the contemplative world of the spirit. It affords children the opportunity to seek out that more primitive, but for them decidedly superior, knowledge which goes far beyond the visible and sensible world and puts them in contact with spiritual reality. This is the kind of knowing best described as "loving."

It is now the eighth day since the prince and the pilot met, and their water supply is gone. The two set out in search of water and find the mysterious well in the middle of the Sahara. The little prince reminds the pilot that he promised to draw him a muzzle for his sheep so that his flower, for whom he is responsible, will be safe. The pilot, now with his thirst satisfied, wonders why he is suddenly seized with a sense of grief. After he has completed a pencil sketch of the muzzle and gives it to the boy his heart is torn. He says, "You have plans I do not know about." It is then that he realizes that it was not by chance when they first met that the boy was "strolling along like that, all alone, a thousand miles from any inhabited region? You were on your way back to the place where you landed?" (80).

When he presses the little prince further, the boy puts him off and tells him to return to his plane and work on the engine, then to return to this place the following evening. With sadness and trepidation that something dreadful is soon to happen, the pilot returns to the plane: "I was not reassured. I remembered the fox. One runs the risk of weeping a little, if one lets himself be tamed" (81).

Tears, like laughter, are a strange phenomenon of human behavior. Things of wonder, they frequently come suddenly and unbidden from the deep mysterious regions of the self most often symbolized as the heart. As his tears flow, the pilot is no longer just a listener to the story of the little prince, but a participant. He can now say of his own grief what he said earlier about the boy's tears: "It is such a secret place, the land of tears" (28).

When he returns the next day the aviator sees the little prince sitting atop an old stone wall, and as he comes closer he can hear that the boy is speaking to someone whom he can neither see nor hear. Eventually, and with great alarm, he sees that it is a deadly snake. To the little prince it is *the* snake, the same one he came upon when he first arrived on Earth. The little prince, like the reader, knew that he would meet the snake again, and all along he has both wished and feared it. Thus Saint-Exupéry sheds light on the wonder and mystery of death. There is always a fear of the unknown. Fear is not something to be eradicated; it is one of the hurdles of life to be faced and dealt with by both child and adult, each in his own way.

As mentioned earlier, the snake is not a symbol of evil, a villain to be hissed. The significance at this juncture is that the boy, with forethought and willingness, even with resolution, has come here to keep his appointment with death. The snake is but a piece of the circumstance.

When he was fifteen Saint-Exupéry witnessed another young boy calmly keeping his rendezvous with death—his brother, François, two years his junior. Early one morning he was awakened by his brother's nurse, who said that François was asking for him. He found François obviously in great pain, but calm and resigned to death. He called for his brother so that he could make his will, Saint-Exupéry remembers:

> this younger brother who was to die in twenty minutes . . . confided to my care . . . a toy steam engine, a bicycle, and a rifle.
>
> Man does not die. Man imagines that it is death he fears; but what he fears is the unforeseen, the explosion. What man fears is himself, not death. There is no death when you meet death. When the body sinks into death, the essence of man is revealed. Man is

a knot, a web, a mesh into which relationships are tied. Only those relationships matter. The body is an old crack that nobody will miss. I have never known a man to think of himself when dying. Never. (*FA*, 182–83)

Surely Antoine was revisiting with his younger brother when writing the final pages of *The Little Prince*. He steadfastly rejected all advice from his publisher, who counseled him against including the death of the boy protagonist.

Death has always been a difficult subject to handle in discussions with children. Adults are usually fortified with the best of biological answers for reasonable questions, but children do not always ask reasonable questions, and there is little to signify that they expect reasonable answers. So the child all too often continues to search for answers to this natural mystery, until one day perhaps it rises as a spectre, so that the child turns and flees, never having seen death for what it truly is.

The Little Prince is not an attempt to supplant the child's fear of death. Neither is it a sermon exhorting boys and girls to be good because of the rewards and punishments of an afterlife. It is, rather, an expression of Saint-Exupéry's firm conviction that life, as we come to know it, has meaning only because of death, and that the two are one. He assumes both that this is a major concern for children and that they are capable of understanding it in their own way. His story does console, nevertheless, for in it he pronounces quite clearly that goodness and love are a natural part of all creation and all experience—even those things and events which may appear to be grotesque, sorrowful, or painful. The young reader who comes to *The Little Prince* is not whisked away into a fairyland of escape, but rather into a place of more intense reality. Here she or he will not find things, but the mystical meaning of things, the intuitive music of things, the soul of things.

The pilot realizes clearly that something extraordinary is happening; that his little friend is rushing headlong toward an abyss from which he can do nothing to restrain him: "I felt myself frozen by the sense of something irreparable. And I knew that I could not bear the thought of never hearing that laughter anymore" (84). The little prince consoles him by reminiscing about the many things they have shared during their short time together. And then he says: "And when your sorrow is comforted (time soothes all sorrows) you will be content that you have known me. You will always be my friend" (85).

The tears and the laughter found in *The Little Prince* are called forth; they are designed, not accidental. Saint-Exupéry would not have children avoid the pain that is sometimes exacted by love; instead, he wants them to recognize that it is an essential nourishment for the soul. Anyone who has not wept has not truly lived.

When the time comes the little prince slips away to meet the snake by himself. The aviator succeeds in catching up to him as he is walking along with a quick and resolute step. The boy says: "It was wrong of you to come. You will suffer. I shall look as if I were dead; and that will not be true. . . . You understand . . . It is too far. I cannot carry this body with me. It is too heavy . . . it will be like an abandoned old shell. There is nothing sad about old shells" (86–87).

His last thought is not of himself:

> "You know—my flower . . . I am responsible for her. And she is so weak! She is naive! She has four thorns, of no use at all, to protect her against all the world." . . .
>
> He still hesitated a little; then he got up. He took one step. . . .
>
> There was nothing but a flash of yellow close to the ankle. he remained motionless for an instant. He did not cry out. He fell gently as a tree falls. There was not even any sound, because of the sand. (88–89)

Pain and suffering, of course, are realities of life that adults wish to spare children. One could argue, however, that true education requires that such feelings be part of the curriculum. This is especially true if we accept the notion that it is with the heart that one sees rightly those invisible matters of consequence. John Keats put it well: "Call the world if you please the Vale of Soul Making. I say Soul Making, Soul as distinguished from an Intelligence. There may be intelligences or sparks of the divinity in millions—but they are not souls till they acquire identities, till each one is personally itself . . . . Do you not see how necessary a world of Pains and troubles is to school an intelligence and make it a Soul? A place where the heart must feel and suffer in a thousand different ways. Not merely is the Heart a Horn Book, it is the mind's Bible, it is the mind's experience . . . as various as the *Lives* of men—so various too become their souls."[3]

Saint-Exupéry, in an April 1943 letter to his wife, attempts to explain why he is returning to the war, when he knows only too well that he is fit neither physically nor psychologically for combat flying:

> I'm off to the war. I cannot bear to be far from those who are hungry. I know only one way to be at peace with my conscience and that is to suffer as much as possible—to seek the greatest possible suffering. That will certainly be granted to me—a man unable, without physical pain, to carry a five-pound package, get out of bed, or pick up a handkerchief from the floor. . . . I'm not going off to die. I'm going off to suffer and in that way be close to my people. (*WW*, 121)

France, for Saint-Exupéry, is not a place on a map, nor a political entity. It is not a matter of slogans, however patriotic or inspiring. France is *home*. It is mother, Léon Werth, the hills of Provence—real people; a living, breathing landscape. This is the France to which the traveler yearns to return, and for which the warrior is willing to die.

Saint-Exupéry lives story. Concepts do not move men to tears, nor to laughter, nor to action. It was impossible for him to write if he was not at the same time involved in consequential matters of his time. One cannot separate the aviator-warrior from the writer; all three professions are carried on simultaneously, and each feeds into the other. His writing, be it story or essay, is a contemplation of not only his history, but also his present experience—a continuous mixture of thought and feeling, matter and spirit.

In dealing with true matters of consequence, one doesn't have the luxury of standing aloof and applying only the cool logic of reason and objectivity and law. These are indeed matters that try not men's minds but their souls, their very being. Errors on the blackboard of reason can be erased and one can start afresh. Not so with matters of the heart, for when things go wrong there the pain that results is deeply felt, leaving slow-healing scars.

The love of place that inspires Saint-Exupéry to defend France and the little prince to return to his planet arises from feelings for the loved ones who represent those places. For the prince, it is his rose; for the author, the major figures are Léon Werth and his mother.

The book is dedicated to Léon Werth. We find all that is essential to understand Saint-Exupéry's strong feelings of friendship in a few letters, and in his public *Letter to a Hostage*, which is also addressed to Werth. We don't need a great deal of biographical data, because in friendship "that which is essential is invisible to the eye."

In *Letter to a Hostage* Saint-Exupéry, stationed in North Africa during the war, recalls his friendship with Werth: "if I inhabited a still living planet, it was because of a few friends left behind me somewhere in the French night. . . . My country was enfolded in them, and through them it lived on inside of me. . . . the man who haunts my memory tonight is fifty years old. He is ill. He is a Jew. How will he survive the German terror?" (*WW*, 109–10).

He then goes on to describe the spiritual bonding of this friendship, focusing on an afternoon the two friends spent leisurely at a café on the banks of the Saône river at Fleurville. Prior to the description he writes:

> How does life build the vital currents that we live from? Where does the magnetic force that pulls me toward this friend's house originate? What are the essential moments that made this presence into a vital pole for me? What are the secret events that mold particular affections, and through them, love of country?
>
> How little stir the real miracles cause! How simple are the most vital events! There is so little to say about the instant that I want to recall that I have to relive it in a dream and speak to this friend. (*WW*, 110)

Upon finishing his description, he acknowledges his inability to snare the essential elements of the experience in words: "My feeble words will allow the truth to escape. . . . Very often the essential is weightless" (*WW*, 112).

Earlier, in a letter to Werth dated February 1940, Saint-Exupéry begins by sharing, as in a friendly chat, his every day life with his flying group. He then goes on to say: "I'd like you to know what in fact you know already; I very much need you, because first of all I think you're the one I love best of all my friends, and also because you're my conscience. I think I apprehend things as you do and you teach me well. I often have long discussions with you and—I'm not being partial—I nearly always agree that you're right" (*WW*, 40). In reading this one thinks not only of the rose, the object of affection, but also of the fox.

Saint-Exupéry often comments on the limitations of language in expressing the spiritual essence of experience. This problem is probably at the root of why for some time he toyed with the idea of writing a fairy tale. It was not just the desire to express himself in a form best suited for children, but rather to choose a form that makes it necessary to pare off the layers of adult experience and get at the mythopoeic, innocent core of childhood experience. Like Andersen, whom he read in preparation, and in the words of C. S. Lewis, he selected the fairy tale because "sometimes fairy stories may say best what's to be said."[4]

The uniqueness of Saint-Exupéry's fairy tale lies in its style, the product of his rare combination of imagination and close observation. He is both a dreamer and a doer. As an observer, he looks at the wonder of things, so that small everyday things take on a surprising magnitude and grandeur.

His style might be appropriately described as *quiet*. It is as though the rugged discipline that he found so necessary for survival as a pioneer of aviation spills over into his writing. His is a simple matter-of-fact approach, stripped bare of all sentimentalism and histrionics. He sees miracles wherever he looks—in the workings of a carburetor, in the laughter of a child. It is as though he expected to find them there. Though *The Little Prince* lies in the realm of fancy, the reader always gets the impression that the author is saying, "This is really the way things are."

In almost all of his writing, Saint-Exupéry is, in some way, a part of his own narrative. Here in the fairy-tale form he accomplishes it through the first-person narration of the story's aviator. As a writer he incessantly snips away at nonessentials, always striving to have the written word lay bare those intangibles of the spirit that are so difficult to identify for oneself, much less verbalize for others.

It is not an overstatement, I think, to say that *The Little Prince* is a culmination of his efforts in this movement toward simple directness. There is nothing harsh about the style. It contains the calm severity of the ascetic, accepting even pain and death as matters of fact. His style is distinctly his own, developed not primarily through reading the works of others but through hundreds of toil-filled hours of writing. No doubt many readers were surprised when they first learned that Saint-Exupéry had written a fairy tale, but now, looking back at his entire literary output, it is evident that his style, as well as the thoughts he wished to convey, were moving him toward this new medium.

Unlike many fanciful tales, *The Little Prince* contains no long sweeping sentences. The story is presented as a simple statement of fact. Indeed, even the adult reader often wonders whether Saint-Exupéry may have actually had some such imaginative experience in the desert, following his crash in 1935. The dialogue, too, is simple and direct. There is constant repetition, but never monotony. The repetitive phrases create a whispered cadence that is particularly appropriate for a story filled with mystery and secrets. It is in no way like the dull drill of memorizing facts. Facts can be forgotten—secrets, never.

Even the form presents a duality that permits *The Little Prince* to be received differently by children and adults. For the younger reader it is indeed a fairy tale. For the more mature reader it may also be an allegorical conte, reminiscent of Rabelais or La Fontaine. Yet, strangely enough, the allegorical structure does not intrude on the younger reader's enjoyment of the fairy tale. Each exists in itself, but also within the other. Perhaps, in this sense, *The Little Prince* is the only one of its kind, and, for that reason, is so very difficult to categorize or compare with other works of fantasy in children's literature.

It is the fairy tale mode, however, that predominates. The fairy tale is a more pure story, free from the one-to-one comparisons of allegory. It demands more of the writer than does allegory, because in order to commit it to paper one must reach deeply into the recesses of oneself, from where it takes more than cleverness or facility with words to bring the story forth. There is nothing confusing about such thoughts for children, for they require the kind of reasoning where analysis and intuition meet—the raw kind of reasoning that needs no schooling. *The Little Prince* is not difficult to understand; it merely requires an intellect smothered in affection.

The Little Prince harkens back to those fairy tales steeped in meaning and morality. It is not a story-sermon; it dares to wrestle with the unfathomable, awesome questions of existence, which age and maturity fail to bring one closer to answering fully. It is a truthful tale, and therein lies its morality. It is not like so many of those moralistic stories that blunt the truly religious sense—untruthful moral tales for the young in which good conduct brings an obvious reward. A tale such as this need not be intellectual or ethical, but merely true; passing in wonder the nature of mysterious things. Ignorance of this kind of fairyland is the punishment of intellectual vanity—the vanity of those adults who have forgotten that education means leading forth, not stuffing in.

The unity of the physical and the spiritual is the basis for all good fairy tales, including this one. The fairy sense is buried in the dark regions of the subconscious, as innate as the religious sense itself. It is the deep-rooted sense that somehow commits us to life, just as intellectualism convinces us of life.

Richard Le Gallienne touched upon the true significance of stories like *The Little Prince* when he wrote:

> The wonder of the world! Perhaps that is the chief business of the fairy tale—to remind us that the world . . . is a rendezvous of radiant forces forever engaged in turning its dust into dreams, ever busy with the transmutation of matter into mind, and mind into spirit. . . . One might even set up, and maintain, the paradox that the fairy tale is the most scientific statement of human life; for of

all statements, it insists on the essential magic of living—the mystery and wonder of being alive, the marvelous happiness, the wondrous sorrow, and the divine expectations.[5]

Having lost his father at age four, Antoine had a very close relationship with his mother. His letters to her, especially those written during the German occupation, are the ones I love to share with young people. In contrast to his other correspondence, they are cryptically brief. One senses that there is a great deal being communicated that goes beyond the words on the page. The brevity only heightens the emotional impact, especially when one is aware of the circumstances during which the letters were composed. They have about them the tone of a young boy away at school who is dreadfully homesick for the one person he yearns to embrace. In January 1944 he ends a very short note, which reached his mother by way of one of the leaders of the Resistance who was parachuted into France:

in a few month's time I hope with all my heart to be folded in your arms, my darling little old Mama, to sit with you by the fire, telling you all I think, trying to contradict you as little as possible, listening to you—you who have been right about everything in life. . . .
I love you dearest Mama.
Antoine (*WW*, 189)

All that would come together finally in *The Little Prince* was mulling around within him during the spring of 1940. And it was often in his letters to his mother that bits and pieces of it would surface: "I don't tell you much about my life; there's not much to tell: dangerous missions, meals, sleep. I'm terribly unsatisfied. The heart needs other employment. I'm very discontented with the preoccupations of the age in which I live. Accepted and experienced danger is not enough to calm one's conscience. The only refreshing spring I can find is in some childhood memories: the smell of burning candles on Christmas Eve. Nowadays, it's the soul that is a desert, dying of thirst" (*WW*, 44).

And in July 1944, the same month in which he would make his last flight, he writes this short note:

My Dearest Mama,

I would like so much to reassure you about me and to be sure
that my letter reaches you. I'm very well. But I'm sad not to have
seen you for so long and I'm worried about you, my darling
Mama. What an unhappy time we live in! . . .
When will it be possible to say to those one loves that one
loves them?
My dearest Mama, love me as I love you.
Antoine (*WW*, 207–8)

Saint-Exupéry's wife, Consuelo, was with him on Long Island,
safely out of harm's way, while he was writing *The Little Prince*.
Otherwise she certainly would be included in the group of loved ones
represented symbolically by the rose. In fact, in personality, she more
than anyone comes closest to the persona of the little prince's flower,
which is revealed in but a few short pages. "She chose her colors with
the greatest care. She dressed herself slowly. She adjusted her petals
one by one. She did not wish to go out into the world all rumpled, like
the field poppies. It was only in the full radiance of her beauty that she
wished to appear. Oh, yes! She was a coquettish creature!" (29).

This passage suggests that the beauty of love is to be found in the
countenance of the lover, not necessarily in the object of affection. The
rose is little more than a vain, selfish little flower, until the reader discovers that she secretly returns the prince's love. When it is time for
him to leave her, she says: "'Of course I love you. . . . It is my fault
that you have not known it all the while. . . . Don't linger like this.
You have decided to go away. Now go!' For she did not want him to
see her crying. She was such a proud flower" (34).

Saint-Exupéry gave a short talk to young Americans on 8
December 1941, the day after the Japanese attacked Pearl Harbor. I
was still in high school at the time and was not present, but I remember well reading the text of his speech the following spring in a copy of
Senior Scholastic and the profound and lasting impression it made
upon me. He opened his talk by speaking from the heart: "I speak to
you as I should like to speak to my own people, who are far away. Be
my friends." And then he got right to the point: "You are ready to

fight for liberty, but you must also explain it. . . . Liberty is not a problem you can separate from others. In order for humans to be free, they must first be humans" (*WW*, 75).

Then he went on to say something that perhaps had been said to me before, but never with such clarity. Like the fox, he shared with me a secret that I had already known, but perhaps because of the discomfort and possible pain connected with it, I had never truly considered its importance. Concerning the secret of being truly human, Saint-Exupéry puts it this way: "The oldest religions discovered [it] long ago. It is the basis of all religious thought. It is the supreme 'trick,' which has been somewhat forgotten since the advent of material progress. That 'trick' is sacrifice. And by sacrifice I mean neither renunciation of all good things of life, nor despair in repentance. By sacrifice I mean a free gift, a gift that demands nothing in return. It is not what you receive that magnifies you, but what you give" (*WW*, 77).

These words, as I say, had a profound and lasting effect on me. They were not necessarily words I wanted to hear, but nevertheless words that I understood and accepted as true for me, even in those early years. A few years later, while I myself was in the Air Force, they were even more indelibly impressed on my maturing consciousness as I read the newly published, *The Little Prince*. And, of course, it was shortly after that I learned that the man who had spoken those words and had written that glorious little book, had lived according to the secrets imparted by the fox as well. He, like his "little fellow," had made the ultimate sacrifice willingly and with much forethought.

At the end of the tale each reader will, I am sure, interpret in his or her own way the death of the little prince. Saint-Exupéry makes clear only one aspect of his own beliefs, and that is that there is more to human existence than is constituted by flesh and blood alone. The spirit is the essential—that which is invisible to the eye—and that lives on, surely in the minds and hearts of others, and perhaps in some other way as well. The little prince speaks for him when he says, "I shall look as if I were dead; and that will not be true" (86).

The author finally hands over his story to the reader, as one would give a present to a friend. He says: "Here then is a great mystery. For you who also love the little prince, and for me, nothing in the universe can be the same if somewhere, we do not know where, a sheep that we never saw has—yes or no?—eaten a rose" (91).

And why is this such an important issue for us? Because now we know how much the little prince has sacrificed and suffered for his beloved rose. It is he—not the rose, nor the sheep—who makes the difference. It is he about whom we are concerned. In the same way we mourn also this aviator who, soon after telling us his tale of mystery, flew off to make a difference in the fate of those he loved.

Though he writes about a real world, Saint-Exupéry hasn't constructed a plot and created a cast of characters from a setting familiar to everyone. He sets forth with a petite stranger, an alien, into a strange land where the signposts are enigmatic. He then dares the reader to accompany him on his journey into unchartered climes. A story world such as this is one best suited for pondering the inner mysteries of one's self. Sociological writing is limited to expeditions of discovery and knowing that can be verified and demonstrated within a community. It dare not, indeed it cannot, venture into a world beyond the apprehension of reason alone.

Many realistic stories presented to preadolescent and adolescent readers revolve around plots and themes that depict the painful struggle of crossing over the line between childhood innocence and adult experience. These stories, for the most part, after a time of initiation and trial, leave the protagonist a bit scarred, but triumphantly ready to get on with whatever the future holds in store. Saint-Exupéry's little work emphasizes, I think, the hidden tragedy of so many of these rites of passage, wherein the garments of innocence and romance are discarded like swaddling clothes, raiments good only for the early years. In their place one dons the entirely new set of clothes, or perhaps armor, of experience and irony, in order to better face the realities that lie ahead. His is a warning not to completely give up, or at least to reclaim if necessary, the power of childhood imagination, and to have confidence in the fresh clear-eyed vision of self-knowledge.

In dreaming we are always better than ourselves, and the world is always better than it is, and surely it is by hypothesizing that things are better that one arrives at making them better. This indeed is what vision means. And it has been said that "without vision the people perish"—not stay as they are, nor even regress, but perish from a deficiency of ideals. A person who is absolutely destitute of imagination can have no ideals, nor charity, nor sympathy, nor creative ability, nor reverence, nor true love.

Saint-Exupéry, the man of action, was also a constant dreamer, and this is the chief reason *The Little Prince* is an important book to place in the way of young readers. The wonders to be found within its pages not only stretch the mind, but set all the faculties on tiptoe, encouraging the reader to catch the bright visions that mysteriously float just out of reach. Here is a writer that converts his private visions into publicly recognizable beauty and universally comprehensible argument. Childish wonder, when confronted with art such as this, is the first step toward not knowledge but wisdom.

Appendix: Approaches to Teaching

In sharing a particular title with children I place the major emphasis on preparing them for the reading experience and then carrying it out, rather than on planning post-reading activities. I have found that the most successful activities that grow out of any reading depend upon how the individual or group responded to the reading itself. Indeed, if they have not responded enthusiastically, no amount of activities after the fact will enhance their appreciation or increase their enjoyment.

My role as a teacher of story is not that of inquisitor—or, if that fails, interpreter, explainer, or declaimer of all that may have been missed by the students. My role is to prepare my students and myself for the reading experience in such a way that they will miss as little as possible. The teacher of literature is more like an impresario, one who presents the work in the best possible circumstances. As teacher I am a representative or agent of the author, who cannot be present; therefore, my job is to prepare for the occasion in a way that I judge will most successfully gain the attention of the particular audience to be engaged—be it an individual, a small group, or an entire class.

I have found *The Little Prince* less suitable for young children. Indeed, since it doesn't have a fast-paced plot or much dramatic action, it perhaps will not, as some critics have noted, be as pleasing to a less discriminating audience of any age. My position, however, is that it is a work uniquely designed to help many youngsters, from upper elementary grades through high school, with the help of a teacher-guide, to move on to a higher plateau of reading enjoyment and appreciation. Here is a work so different in concept and design that it can help erase the many misconceived prejudices they, as well as many adults, hold concerning traditional fairy tales and their modern counterparts.

Perhaps the most unusual feature of *The Little Prince* is that its author chooses to enter his own story. It is not often that one finds an author in a fairy tale of his own making. The fact that the narrator, speaking in the first person, is an aviator is especially significant, since Saint-Exupéry, who certainly could have lived comfortably off the royalties of his books, always considered himself an aviator by profession. In preparing youngsters, especially those who have as yet spurned books of fantasy, for an enthusiastic encounter with *The Little Prince*, I have therefore found it extremely helpful to introduce them to this very unusual pilot-author. Or more accurately, I give Saint-Exupéry the opportunity to introduce himself.

This can be accomplished in a modicum of time and without teacher explanation. There are two brief selections from *Wind, Sand and Stars* that I have consistently found to hold children riveted to their seats during the reading. The first tells of the author's experience of flying through a cyclone off the coast of Argentina, which was physically the most overwhelming experience of his life. The second consists of a few short selected pieces from the chapter describing his crash in the Sahara during his 1935 Paris-to-Saigon flight. These selections not only establish the credentials of the aviator-narrator of *The Little Prince*, but they also help to create a unique tension between the real and the fanciful in the story.

To further promote the students' interest in the unfolding of the story, the teacher may expose them to the historical and personal circumstances of the time in which it was written. This too is easily accomplished, by focusing on the dedication. The dedication to Léon Werth also serves as a preface. In a sense, it is to Werth that Saint-Exupéry is telling his story, and the rest of us are given the privilege of listening in. Children of middle-school age and older are pretty well acquainted with what was happening in Europe, and especially in France, during the 1940s, when the book was being written. By merely sharing one or two excerpts from Saint-Exupéry's writings that reflect the close friendship that existed between these two men separated by war, one can establish an appropriate emotional atmosphere for the reading to follow. This, along with the realistic opening of the story, also prompts a young reader, from the very outset, to consider what reflections of reality may be uncovered during this flight into fancy.

As for the reading of the story, the book lends itself to easy classroom management. Each of the chapters averages less than three pages of print, but of course the illustrations, since they are not mere adornments, must be "read" as well. The first section (7–34), in which the initial meeting takes place and the aviator gradually learns about the little prince's life, and the second section (35–55), detailing the prince's visits to the six planets, are episodic and therefore may be divided into discrete groupings as the teacher sees fit. The little prince's early experiences on Earth, his initial meeting with the snake, and his coming upon the rose-garden (56–64) can be accomplished in one sitting. The encounter with the fox (64–71), because of its importance, should be read on its own; so too, the search for the well (71–81). The final pages and the prologue should also be read at one sitting because of the high drama that takes place.

A reading of *The Little Prince* may appropriately be integrated with a variety of themes or topics that a group may be considering in their other studies: war (World War II in particular), the environment, aviation, the hero, moral responsibility, death, etc. It may also be a stepping-stone for some youngsters to better appreciate that tales of fantasy can have a direct relationship to their experiential world. Pairing the book with realistic stories sometimes helps to break the stereotype that equates fairy tales with nursery stories.

A book that I have often paired with *The Little Prince* is *The Big Wave*, by Pearl Buck. In the preface to her book, entitled "A Letter from the Author," Buck writes: "I can remember quite well how this book began. It was during the war and I saw that many children were afraid, even American children. They were not used to the idea of death. They thought death only comes to old people. But during the war they learned that death comes also to the young. . . . I saw them afraid. . . . So I wrote this book *The Big Wave*. . . . Let it be read, let it be seen, that life is stronger than death, and we need not be afraid."[1]

There is much to be frightened of in the lives of many children today, and to help deal with it they need succor of the spirit as well as the body. Stories like these two, one fanciful and one realistic, can take them for a little while out of their immediate surroundings and off to the vastness and bleakness of the Sahara, or to a tiny fishing village on an island off the coast of Japan that is always in threat of being swept away by a tidal wave. There is always the very good possibility that many of them will find hope and consolation from their reading, even though they may not be consciously aware of it, nor capable sometimes of adequately expressing it in words. They may come away from the books having enjoyed each for the story itself. However, in that alone there is a great humanizing factor. As C. S. Lewis says: "Literary experience heals the wound, without undermining the privilege of individuality. . . . In reading great literature I become a thousand men and yet remain myself. Like the night sky in the Greek poem, I see with a myriad eyes, but it is still I who see. Here, as in worship, in love, in moral action, and in knowing, I transcend myself and am never more myself than when I do."[2] Saint-Exupéry could have easily written those words himself.

Both *The Little Prince* and *The Big Wave* have about them a quality and atmosphere of transcendence. Each in its own way touches upon the coming into and the leave-taking from this world, and upon some of the wonders experienced by just being in it. Children's own concept of the world is steeped with imagination, wonders, and mystery; they perform their own rituals and collect their own talismans. Why then should books that are infused with these same elements be beyond their abilities?

This quality of transcending is what also qualifies *The Little Prince* as a classic in children's literature. Solidly founded in the world in which Saint-Exupéry lived, rooted deeply in his own experience, his fairy tale transcends time and place so that it will continue to speak to readers 100 years hence—50 have already gone by. It has not and will not lose its relevancy. All classics join the ranks of Homer, no matter how humble in comparison.

I feel that I must interject a word here concerning the vocabulary one uses in talking about books like *The Little Prince*. I have found for some time now that many teachers are actually frightened to use such words as *spirit*, *soul*, and *sacred*, lest they be accused of inappropriately injecting religion into the classroom. But these words have always been part of the essential vocabulary of writers and artists. Some of the quotes I've used in this book, like those of Frost and Keats, are fine examples. One need only go to Bartlett's *Familiar Quotations* to see the extent to which these words are vital and legitimate descriptors of artistic expression. As disciplines grow more compartmentalized, the vocabulary of literature is minimized. The role of educators is to help build the student's vocabulary, not constrict it. If a student can better appreciate the full measure of a word's context, then perhaps a word like *myth* might no longer be confined to being synonymous with *falsehood*. On this subject, I urge teachers of literature to look to the poets and storytellers themselves for guidance. Too often they are the ones to whom we pay the least attention.

Several times I have shared *The Little Prince* with youngsters while they were also reading biographies on their own. I did this in order to demonstrate that when it comes to authors and poets of integrity, it is their work that tells us most about their inner, "invisible" selves and those issues which for them are "matters of consequence." In the case of Saint-Exupéry this is especially true. That is why, in the preceding chapters, I included connecting links between his fairy tale and his other works, and indeed the manner in which he lived his life. Aviator, writer, patriot, this remarkable person took an active role in the affairs of his time, and yet his writing reveals to us clearly that he was also constantly dealing with matters that far outreached the 40-odd years of his life. The reason his little fairy tale has such dramatic resonance is that his words come from the heart, the spirit—and so they still have meaning for us today.

Over a semester a teacher may want to include *The Little Prince* with a variety of other works under the broad category of fantasy. In such a context, students have the opportunity not only to appreciate the richness of the genre, but also to discover that each title will elicit a different reader response. The teacher will not have difficulty finding quality titles to represent each sub-group: for example, science fiction with *Wrinkle in Time*, quest stories with *The Hobbit*, or nonsense with Norton Juster's *The Phantom Tollbooth*.

The Little Prince also lends itself to student dramatization. With the aviator as narrator, the dialogue between the characters can be taken almost verbatim from the book. As for media presentations, I have found few that capture the spirit of the original. Youngsters for the most part find the Paramount film production to be pleasant enough, but I would leave the choice of including its use up to others. Hollywood seems to have an incessant need to convert children's classics into musicals when bringing them to the screen. In the case of *The Little Prince* the effort is disappointing. Several videos supposedly based upon Saint-Exupéry's boy prince have found their way into the market. They are purely exploitive. Over the years there have been several high-quality recorded and taped readings by well-known actors, the most recent of which features Louis Jourdan.[3]

The media piece I have used most often is a recording in French with the well-known actor Gerard Philipe in the role of the aviator.[4] It gives a wonderful cadence and muted sound to the reading, and it can be easily followed by children who know the story and have the English text in front of them. It demonstrates also that one may drop the little prince's visits to other planets, focus on his adventures on Earth and still have a compact, unified, and dramatic story. It illustrates, too, that much more is conveyed in the artistic use of spoken language than in the denotation of the words. Robert Frost emphasizes that sentences must do more than convey a meaning of words, they must convey a meaning of sound: "catching the conversational tones which are the special property of vital utterances."[5]

In the intermediary role that the teacher plays there is one essential skill that he or she must continually practice: the art of reading aloud. For young or inexperienced readers the words of a story, especially one so subtle in nature as *The Little Prince*, must come off the printed page and back into sound. The reader must hear the words even if he or she is reading silently. Teachers may be the only models that some youngsters have in this regard. One cannot read literature by speed-reading methods. Robert Louis Stevenson said it well: "To pass from hearing literature to reading it is to take a great and dangerous step. With not a few, I think a large proportion of their pleasure then comes to an end; 'the malady of not marking' overtakes them; they read thence-forward by the eye alone and hear never again the chime of fair words or the march of the stately period."[6]

My final comment is to repeat once more, for emphasis, what I said in my opening to this appendix. Once you have prepared the environment as best you can for a successful reading, let Saint-Exupéry take over. Allow him to take the stage and do the teaching. Writers of integrity want readers to enter into a story and be moved by its substance, not to stand outside it and analyze the craft. That can be done in retrospect. Robert Frost, when he was going off to Amherst to teach undergraduates for the first time, told an interviewer: "I don't want to analyze authors. I want to enjoy them, to know them. I want the boys in the classes to enjoy their books because of what's in them. . . . Let them build up a friendship with the writing world first."[7] If that is true for college students, how much more it holds true for younger readers.

Notes and References

Chapter 1

1. *The Little Prince*, trans. Katherine Woods (New York: Harcourt Brace Jovanovich, 1943); hereafter cited in the text.

2. *Wind, Sand and Stars*, trans. Lewis Galantière (New York: Reynal & Hitchcock, 1939), 306; hereafter cited in the text as *WSS*.

3. *Night Flight*, trans. Stuart Gilbert (New York: Century Co., 1932).

4. Saint-Exupéry, *Flight to Arras*, trans. Lewis Galantière (New York: Reynal & Hitchcock, 1943), 225; hereafter cited in the text as *FA*.

5. "Letter to a Hostage" in *Wartime Writings 1939–1944*, trans. Norah Purcell (New York: Harcourt Brace Jovanovich, 1986), 117–18; hereafter *Wartime Writings 1939–1944* will be cited in the text as *WW*.

6. Curtis Cate, *Antoine de Saint-Exupéry* (New York: G. P. Putnam's Sons, 1970), 137.

Chapter 2

1. Simone Weil, "Morality and Literature," in *The Simone Weil Reader*, ed. George A. Panichas (New York: David McKay Company, 1977), 292.

Chapter 3

1. Cate, *Antoine de Saint-Exupéry*, 461.

2. John Chamberlain, review of *The Little Prince*, *New York Times*, 6 April 1943, 19.

3. Florence Bethune Sloan, "Let's Read Now," *Christian Science Monitor*, 30 August 1943.

4. Katharine S. White, review of *The Little Prince*, *New Yorker*, 29 May 1943, 65.

5. Anne Carroll Moore, review of *The Little Prince*, *Horn Book Magazine*, May–June 1943, 166.

6. Cate, *Antoine de Saint-Exupéry* , 464.

7. P. L. Travers, "Across the Sand Dunes to the Prince's Star," *New York Herald Tribune Weekly Book Review*, 11 April 1943, 5.

8. Graham Greene, "The Lost Childhood," in *The Lost Childhood and Other Essays* (New York: Viking Press, 1951), 13–17.

9. P. L. Travers, "Only Connect," in *Only Connect: Readings on Children's Literature*, ed. Sheila Egoff, G. T. Stubbs, and L. F. Ashley (New York: Oxford University Press, 1969), 183–206.

10. Victor E. Graham, "Religion and Saint-Exupéry's *Le Petit Prince*," *Canadian Modern Language Review*, 15, no. 3 (1959): 11.

11. Philip Mooney, S. J., "*The Little Prince*: A Story for Our Time," *America*, 20 December 1969, 611.

12. André Maurois, "Antoine de Saint-Exupéry," ed. and trans. Renaud Bruce, in *From Proust to Camus: Profiles of Modern French Writers*, (New York: Weidenfeld and Nicolson, 1967), 215.

13. Robert Price, "*Pantagruel* and *Le Petit Prince*," *Symposium*, 26 February 1968, 179.

14. Laurence Gagnon, "Webs of Concern: Heidegger, *The Little Prince* and *Charlotte's Web*," *Children's Literature: Annual of the Modern Language Association Seminar on Children's Literature and the Children's Literature Association* 2 (1973): 61–66.

15. Bonner Mitchell, "*Le Petit Prince* and 'Citadelle': Two Experiments in the Didactic Style," *French Review*, April 1960, 454–61.

16. James E. Higgins, "*The Little Prince*: A Legacy," *Elementary English*, December 1960, 514–15.

17. James E. Higgins, *Beyond Words: Mystical Fancy in Children's Literature* (New York: Teachers College Press, 1970), 112.

18. Maxwell A. Smith, *Knight of the Air: The Life and Works of Antoine de Saint-Exupéry* (Pageant Press, 1956), 265.

19. Anne Morrow Lindbergh, "Adventurous Writing," *Saturday Review of Literature*, 14 October 1939, 9.

20. Zena Sutherland and May Hill Arbuthnot, *Children and Books*, 8th ed. (Glenview, Ill.: Scott, Foresman, 1990), 243.

21. Charlotte S. Huck, Susan Helper and Janet Hickman, *Children's Literature in the Elementary School*, 5th ed. (New York: Harcourt Brace Jovanovich, 1993), 400.

22. Allan W. Davis, "Contradiction and Paradox as a Mode of Thought and a Stylistic Device in Saint-Exupéry" (Ph.D. diss., University of Missouri, 1981), Ann Arbor: University of Michigan, 81-71413.

23. Paul Webster, *Antoine de Saint-Exupéry: The Life and Death of the Little Prince* (London: Macmillan, 1993).

24. Eugen Drewermann, *Discovering the Royal Child Within: A Spiritual Psychology of "The Little Prince"* (New York: Crossroad Publishing Co., 1993).

25. Barnet De Ramus, *From Juby to Arras: Engagement in Saint-Exupéry* (New York: University Press of America, 1990).

26. Joy Robinson, *Antoine de Saint-Exupéry*, Twayne's World Authors Series (Boston: Twayne Publishers, 1984).

Chapter 4

1. Plato, "Phaedrus," in *The Dialogues of Plato; Great Books of the Western World*, vol. 7 (Chicago: Encyclopedia Britannica, 1952), 126.

2. Rollo May, *Power and Innocence* (New York: W.W. Norton, 1972), 48–49.

3. André Maurois, quoted in Eliot Gilbert Fay, "Saint-Exupéry in New York," *Modern Language Notes* 61 (November 1946): 461.

4. Anne Carroll Moore, "The Three Owl Notebook," *Horn Book* 19 (May 1943): 164.

5. *Wisdom of the Sands*, trans. Stuart Gilbert (New York: Harcourt, Brace, 1950); hereafter cited in the text as *WS*.

6. E. B. White, *Stuart Little* (New York: Harper & Row, 1945), 131.

7. William Saroyan, *The Human Comedy* (New York: Harper, Brace & World, 1943), 5.

8. Charles Dickens, *Hard Times* (New York: W.W. Norton, 1966), 1.

9. Virginia Woolf, "The Supernatural in Fiction," in *Granite and Rainbow* (New York: Harcourt, Brace, 1958), 64.

10. Thomas Hood, "I Remember, I Remember," in *The Poetical Works of Thomas Hood*, Vol. 1 (New York: Merrill and Baker, n.d.), 206.

Chapter 5

1. William Blake, *The Poetry and Prose of William Blake*, ed. David V. Erdman (New York: Doubleday, 1965), 512.

2. D. H. Lawrence, "Snake" in *The Complete Poems of D.H. Lawrence*, vol. 1 (New York: Viking, 1964), 350.

3. François Marie Arouet de Voltaire, *Candide or Optimism*, 2d ed., trans. and ed. Robert M. Adams (New York: Norton, 1966), 75.

4. J. R. R. Tolkien, "On Fairy-Stories," in *The Tolkien Reader* (New York: Ballantine Books, 1966), 66.

Chapter 6

1. Thomas Stearns Eliot, *Points of View* (London: Faber and Faber, 1941), 76–77.

2. Tolkien, *The Tolkien Reader*, 84.

3. Walt Whitman, "When Lilacs Last in the Dooryard Bloom'd," in *Leaves of Grass* (New York: Bantam Books, 1983), 264.

4. Karl Jaspers, *Reason and Anti-Reason in Our Time* (New Haven: Yale University Press, 1952), 59.

5. George MacDonald, *The Princess and the Goblin* (New York: Macmillan, 1951), 181.

Chapter 7

1. E. B. White, *Charlotte's Web* (New York: Harper & Row, 1952), 184.

2. Gilbert Keith Chesterton, "The Toy Theatre," in *Tremendous Trifles* (New York: Sheed and Ward, 1955), 119.

3. John Keats, "Letter to His Brother George and Sister Georgiana," 21 April 1819, in *Selected Poems and Letters of John Keats* (Boston: Houghton Mifflin, 1959), 288–89.

4. C. S. Lewis, "Sometimes Fairy Stories May Say Best What's to Be Said," *New York Times Book Review*, 18 Nov. 1956, 3.

5. Richard Le Gallienne, "Concerning Fairy-Tales," in *Attitudes and Avowals* (New York: John Lane Co., 1910), 36–37.

Appendix: Approaches to Teaching

1. Pearl S. Buck, *The Big Wave* (New York: Scholastic, 1960).

2. C. S. Lewis, *An Experiment in Criticism* (Cambridge: Cambridge University Press, 1961), 140–41.

3. *The Little Prince* (audiotape) (New York: Harper Audio), CPN 1695 Caedmon.

4. *The Little Prince* (recorded in French) (Los Angeles: Everest Records), #S385278.

5. *Interviews with Robert Frost*, ed. E. C. Latham (New York: Holt, Rinehart and Winston, 1966), 25.

6. Robert Louis Stevenson, "Random Memories," in *Sketches, Criticisms, Lay Morals and Other Essays*, vol. 24 of *Works* (New York: Scribner's, 1923), 247.

7. *Interviews with Robert Frost*, 49.

Selected Bibliography

Primary Sources

Books

Night Flight. Translated by Stuart Gilbert. New York: Century Co., 1932. Reprint. San Diego: Harcourt, Brace, 1974.

Southern Mail. Translated by Stuart Gilbert. New York: Smith & Hass, 1933. Reprint. Translated by Curtis Cate. San Diego: Harcourt, Brace, 1967.

Wind, Sand and Stars. Translated by Lewis Galantière. New York: Reynal & Hitchcock, 1939. Reprint. San Diego: Harcourt, Brace, 1992.

Flight to Arras. Translated by Lewis Galantière. New York: Reynal & Hitchcock, 1942. Reprint. San Diego: Harcourt, Brace, 1969.

Airman's Odyssey. Translated by Gilbert Stuart and Lewis Galantière. New York: Reynal & Hitchcock, 1942. Reprint. San Diego: Harcourt, Brace, 1984. Contains *Wind, Sand and Stars*, *Night Flight*, and *Flight to Arras*.

The Little Prince. Translated by Katherine Woods. New York: Harcourt Brace Jovanovich, 1943. Reprint. San Diego: Harcourt, Brace, 1982.

Wisdom of the Sands. Translated by Stuart Gilbert. New York: Harcourt, Brace, 1949.

A Sense of Life. Translated by Adrienne Foulke. New York: Funk & Wagnalls, 1965.

Wartime Writings, 1939–1944. Translated by Norah Purcell. Introduction by Anne Morrow Lindbergh. New York: Harcourt Brace Jovanovich, 1986. Reprint. San Diego: Harcourt, Brace, 1990.

Articles

"Letter to Young Americans." *Senior Scholastic*, 25 May 1942. Translated by Lewis Galantière. Included in *Wartime Writings 1939–1944*, as "A Message to Young Americans," 75–79.

"An Open Letter to Frenchmen Everywhere." *New York Times Magazine*, 29 November 1942, 7ff.

"Letter to a Hostage." In *Wartime Writings 1939–1944*, 103–19.

Secondary Sources

Books

Bréaux, Adèle. *Saint Exupéry in America, 1942–43*. Rutherford, N.J.: Fairleigh Dickinson University Press, 1971. A memoir by Saint-Exupéry's English teacher during the time he was writing *The Little Prince*.

Bree, Germaine, and Margaret Otis Guiton. *Age of Fiction: The French Novel from Gide to Camus*. New Brunswick, N.J.: Rutgers University Press, 1957. Section on Saint-Exupéry (193–203) places him among the other leading French writers of his time.

Cate, Curtis. *Antoine de Saint-Exupéry: His Life and Times*. New York: Putnam, 1970. The biography with which most Americans are familiar, but by no means a definitive work. Written in a popular style and including many anecdotes.

Children's Literature Review. Vol. 10. Detroit: Gale Research Company, 1986. Includes a fine selection of excerpts from reviews, criticism, and commentary concerning *The Little Prince* (137–61).

Migéo, Marcel. *Saint-Exupéry*. Translated by Herma Briffault. New York: McGraw-Hill, 1960. An engaging reminiscence by a pilot who flew with Saint-Exupéry during his military service.

Robinson, Joy. *Antoine de Saint-Exupéry*. Twayne's World Authors Series. Boston: Twayne Publishers, 1984. A scholarly work in which the author's affection for the writing of Saint-Exupéry shows through. A thorough and well-documented reference.

Rumbold, Richard, and Margaret Stewart. *The Winged Life*. New York: McKay, n.d. Two British fliers share their enthusiasm for the life and work of the French author-pilot they so admired.

Schiff, Stacy. *Saint-Exupéry: A Biography*. New York: Alfred A. Knopf, 1994. A thoroughly researched biography that is a detailed account of Saint-Exupéry's private life.

Smith, Maxwell A. *Knight of the Air.* New York: Pageant Press, 1956. A distinctive biography that brings Saint-Exupéry to life through interviews with those who knew him best.

Articles

Balakian, Nona. "Poet of the Air—and Earth." In *Critical Encounters,* 142–45. New York: Bobbs-Merrill, 1978.

Daniel, Vera J. "Antoine de Saint-Exupéry." *Contemporary Review* 190 (August 1953): 97–100.

Fay, Eliot Gilbert. "Saint-Exupéry in New York." *Modern Language Notes* 61 (November 1946): 458–63.

Frohock, Wilbur Merrill. "Saint-Exupéry: The Poet as Novelist." In *Style and Temper: Studies in French Fiction,* 31–44. Cambridge: Harvard University Press, 1967.

Galantière, Lewis. "Antoine de Saint-Exupéry." *Atlantic Monthly* 179 (April 1947): 133–41. Reminiscences by one of Saint-Exupéry's English translators.

Jung, Carl Gustav. "The Phenomenology of the Spirit in Fairy Tales." In *Spirit and Nature,* Bolinger Series 30. New York: Pantheon Books, 1954. 1:3–48. Must reading for anyone who wishes to consider the significance of fairy tales.

Knight, Everett W. "Saint-Exupéry." In *Literature Considered as Philosophy,* 160–85. New York: Macmillan, 1958.

Lindbergh, Anne Morrow. "Adventurous Writing." *Saturday Review of Literature,* 14 October 1939, 8–9. See also her introduction to *Wartime Writings 1939–1944,* ix–xvii.

Maurois, André. "Antoine de Saint-Exupéry." In *From Proust to Camus,* translated by Carl Morse and Renaud Bruce, 204–23. New York: Doubleday, 1966. Places Saint-Exupéry with his contemporaries.

Milligan, E. E. "Saint-Exupéry and Language." *Modern Language Journal* 39 (May 1955): 249–51.

Peyre, Henri. "Antoine de Saint-Exupéry." In *French Novelists of Today,* 154–79. New York: Oxford University Press, 1967. Measures Saint-Exupéry's work alongside that of other writers of this century.

Pritchett, V. S. "Antoine de Saint-Exupéry: Lost in the Stars." In *Lasting Impressions,* 123–27. New York: Random House, 1990. An insightful commentary on Migéo's intimate biography by England's premier man of letters.

Tolkien, J. R. R. "On Fairy-Stories." In *The Tolkien Reader,* 3–84. New York: Ballantine Books, 1966. A classic piece concerning the nature of fairy stories, in particular how they connect with children.

Index

About the Author

Jim Higgins is a native New Yorker. After World War II he attended college on the G.I. Bill, receiving a B.A. in English from St. Bonaventure University, a B.L.S. from St. John's University, and both a master's and a doctorate from Teachers College, Columbia University.

His first teaching assignment was in a Jesuit prep school in Brooklyn, where he also filled in as a librarian. In 1953 he became a teacher-librarian in the Levittown, New York, public schools. In 1965 he joined the faculty of the State University of New York at Stony Brook, where he received the Outstanding Teacher Award from the graduating classes of 1969 and 1970. He is now professor emeritus from Queens College, City University of New York, where he spent 25 years in the Department of Elementary and Early Childhood Education. He resides in Stony Brook, New York.